MW00603639

Where
in the World ...

READ, WRITE, SPEAK, LISTEN, AND VISIT
30 GREAT PLACES
ON PLANET EARTH

Anne Siebert
Raymond C. Clark

Revised First Edition

Pro Lingua  **Associates**

Pro Lingua Associates, Publishers

P.O. Box 1348
Brattleboro, Vermont 05302 USA
Office: 802-257-7779
Orders: 800-366-4775
Email: info@ProLinguaAssociates.com
WebStore www.ProLinguaAssociates.com
SAN: 216-0579

*At Pro Lingua
our objective is to foster an approach
to learning and teaching that we call* **interplay**,
the **inter**action *of language learners and teachers
with their materials, with the language and culture,
and with each other in active, creative
and productive* **play**.

Acknowledgements

The authors thank the following people for providing stamps and non-English names, greetings, and other expressions: Didier Audon, Vladena Dmitriev, William Eubank, Yukiko Furuta, Ayako Kobayashi, and Yan Zhou.

Copyright © 2007, 2008 by Anne Siebert
ISBN 13: 978-0-86647-286-9 • ISBN 10: 0-86647-286X

COVER PHOTOGRAPH: © YULIYAN VELCHEV; TITLE PAGE: © VASIU / AGENCY: DREAMSTIME.COM

All rights reserved. No part of this publication may be reproduced or transmitted in any form or by any means, electronic, mechanical, photocopying, recording or other, or stored in an information storage or retrieval system without permission in writing from the publisher.

This book was designed by Susannah Clark and Arthur A. Burrows, and printed and bound by Sheridan Books in Ann Arbor, Michigan.

Printed in the United States of America

First edition, second printing, revised 2008. 2500 copies in print.

Contents

The two optional Basic CD's have recordings of the dialogues (A and L), the readings (C), and the pronunciation check chants (J). The tracks are given above. For the two optional Dictation CD's, the tracks are given with the dictations on pages 184-189.

To the Teacher

Where in the World is an integrated skills activity book for beginning-level ESL students. It features visits to 30 well-known places around the world. As the learners "travel" from place to place, the complexity of the language increases until in the last few places, the learners are working at a low-intermediate level. The book can be effectively used with upper elementary school, high school, college and adult learners. In addition to language development, it deals with historical and cultural content, and selected current issues throughout our contemporary world.

The book, in essence, is a vicarious adventure for your students. Some of the places in the book are in your students' native countries, places in which they, of course, take great pride and pleasure. Others are places they would really like to see. It is a book that features interesting, unusual, and beautiful places and different cultures to enjoy, talk about, and learn from.

High-level ESL books on interesting topics are common. But low-level books can also be interesting and enjoyable. This book presents accessible topics and a variety of interactive activities. In addition to the pictures, which are lessons in themselves, the book includes speaking, listening, reading, and writing skills as well as pronunciation practice, vocabulary development, and grammar review. It's all there.

As teachers have long known, understanding and forming questions are among the most difficult challenges for the beginning ESL student. At the very lowest levels of learning, students are required to answer questions such as, "Where were you born?" and "When were you born?" and ask questions such as, "Where is the bus station?"

For that reason, one of the aims of this book is to teach students to ask and to respond to questions, especially to the five W's of *what, where, when, who, why,* and even *how.* When coupled with discussion of interesting historical and natural sites around the world, the task is more enjoyable.

Adding to the interest, each lesson has a choral rap/chant that will have students clapping, "singing," and even "acting out," bringing the house down. The units begin and end with a "phone call" with Igor, who travels around the world with the students. As the lessons progress, the phone calls become increasingly idiomatic — the kind of language that native speakers use in everyday conversation. So until you and your students actually go around the world, enjoy the pictures, travel virtually with Igor — and bon voyage!

Finally, have your students ever brought pictures of their countries to class? Have you noticed the immediate response of other students, the genuine interest and spontaneous questions? "What is this place?" "Where is it?" "Have you been there?" The connection with the pictures and with each other is immediate. And they can't stop talking. It's a teacher's dream. From such experiences, repeated many times over, *Where in the World* was born. • *AS*

How to Use the Book

Introduce the book.
Use the map on page viii to introduce the places and countries in the book. Let the students work in pairs or groups to try to identify the location of the places. Then briefly describe the parts of the book, using the first unit as an example.

Begin with the picture.
Stimulate the students' interest. Get them to say anything they can about it. Ask them questions: What is it? What do you know about this place? Where is it? What's special about it? Has anybody been there? Show its location on the map. Bring in other pictures.

Practice the WH questions.
Use the questions and their responses under the picture. Consult the reading if necessary. Model the WH questions and answers, and then have the students give a response. This reinforces the meaning of the WH questions and also prepares the students for the reading.

A. Where's Igor?
Each dialogue introduces the site. Find out what's going on. Where is Igor? What's he doing there? The dialogue may need to be modeled, then practiced again and again to get the right rhythm and intonation.

Play Part A on the CD (optional).
Have the students listen to part A at least twice. Then have them read along aloud at the same pace to practice the rhythm and intonation of English.

B. Introduce the new words of the text.
Show pictures, explain, act out, and write translations into native languages. Do anything to establish meaning. Say the words and have the students repeat. Add stress marks where necessary.

C. Read the text.
Read to the students. Read slowly, stopping when necessary to explain the content. Let them read with you a second time. Ask for volunteers to read singly. Note that the number at the end of the reading is the number of words in the reading. The readings progress from 50 to 175. The passage is also on the CD.

To the Teacher

D. Answer the questions individually or in pairs.

This is a comprehension check to be sure the students understand the content. Notice that they are asked to respond with a variety of answers (there's more than one way to say true or false).

E. Have the students write answers to the WH questions.

You can also have them practice orally. Student A asks the question. Student B says the answer they have written.

F. Grammar check.

Have the students do this individually. This can be a diagnostic check to see what aspects of the grammar may need more work.

G. Word check.

The words are key words from the reading. Have the students do this individually, then pair up to compare answers. The answers are in the back of the book if they disagree.

H. Dictate sentences.

The sentences are at the end of this book, progressing from short to longer. They are broken into breath groups, usually in groups that correspond to basic English phrase structure: Subject, Verb, Object, Adverbial. Sentences are available on a supplemental CD.

I. Write.

Write a "Wish you were here" postcard. First, write a model paragraph. Point out capitalization and punctuation. Make sure the students practice writing at every lesson, no exceptions. Practice does make perfect. From time to time, copy a blank postcard and have them "send" one to you.

J. Pronunciation check.

The linguistic purpose of this activity is to work on the stress, intonation, and rhythm of English. Model it, clap your hands, stamp your feet, snap your fingers, make some words louder, softer, stretch them out – anything that celebrates the topic that you have studied. Put students in groups and let them compete for the most original presentation. Note that the chant is in two columns so you can have half the class speak the left column and the other half respond with the other column and then switch. Or, just have everybody speak the whole chant. You can also have the students mark the primary stresses.

Where in the World...

K. Talk about it.

In small groups, have a student lead an informal, unstructured conversation about the questions and others that may arise. Students can compare the famous place with places they know about. One person can report to the class on their group's findings.

L. Checking up on Igor.

One more time, let Igor speak about his travels — where he's been and where he's going. Usually there is an "information gap." Discuss it. What's happening? This conversation is also available on the CD.

M. Check the Internet.

This can be an overnight assignment, if the students have access to the Internet. The language on the web sites can be challenging, but the student will find some familiar words, and they can have access to many pictures.

Supplementary Materials and Activities

Review vocabulary from previous lessons from time to time.

Show videos of the famous places, readily available at libraries.

Put up a wall map of the world and chart Igor's progress with pins and thread.

This is one approach to *Where in the World*. Feel free to change, amend, add, and improvise. We'd love to hear what works for you. But keep in mind the most common frustration of beginning-level students, "please, teacher, too fast." So take your time, repeat, review, recycle, reinforce, and learn right along with your students about this great big, beautiful world of ours.

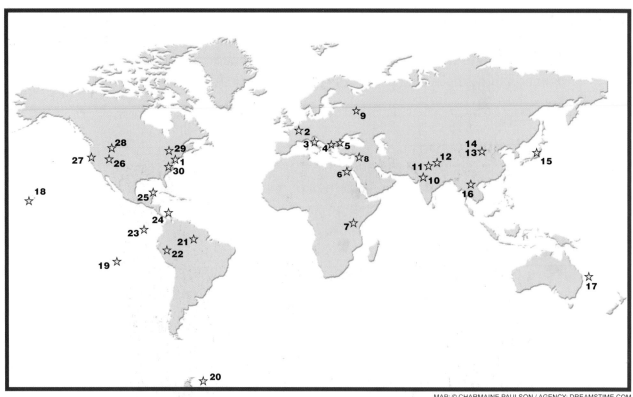

MAP: © CHARMAINE PAULSON / AGENCY: DREAMSTIME.COM

?   Where in the world is...   ?

____ Antarctica

____ Arizona

____ Athens

____ Australia

____ Brazil

____ California

____ Cambodia

____ China

____ Easter Island

____ Galapagos Islands

____ Hawaii

____ India

____ Istanbul

____ Japan

____ Jordan

____ Mexico

____ Moscow

____ Nepal

____ New York

____ Niagara Falls

____ Egypt

____ Panama

____ Paris

____ Peru

____ Rome

____ Tanzania

____ Tibet

____ Washington, D.C.

____ Wyoming

Where in the World...

LADY
LIBERTY

PHOTOGRAPHER: © STEPHEN TROELL | AGENCY: DREAMSTIME.COM

WHAT? the Statue of Liberty　　**WHO? France**

WHERE? New York　　**WHO? America**

WHEN? 1884　　**WHY? a birthday present**

A. Where's Igor?

(rrrrring)

Igor: **Hello!**

You: **Hello, Igor? Where are you?**

Igor: **I'm in New York, New York!**

You: **Really? What are you doing there?**

Igor: **I'm visiting the Statue of Liberty.**

You: **The Statue of Liberty?**

Igor: **Yes, the Statue of Liberty.**

You: **She's big and beautiful, isn't she?**

Igor: **She really is!**

You: **Well, enjoy yourself!**

Igor: **I will! Goodbye.**

B. Do you know these words?

tall _____

beautiful _____

a statue _____

liberty_____

a harbor_____

symbol_____

freedom_____

hope_____

a present _____

C. Read.

The Statue of Liberty is a tall, beautiful woman. She is one of the tallest statues in the world. She is in New York Harbor. She is a symbol of freedom and hope. She was a birthday present from France for America's 100th birthday. Lady Liberty came to America in 1884. (51)

D. Answer: *Yes, it is.* **or** *No, it isn't.*

Example: Is the Statue of Liberty in New York? *Yes, it is.*

1. Is the Statue of Liberty tall? _____

2. Is the Statue of Liberty in France? _____

3. Is the Statue a man? _____

4. Is the Statue a symbol? _____

5. Is the Statue in a harbor? _____

E. Write the answers.

1. What is the Statue of Liberty? _____

   _____

2. Where is the Statue of Liberty? _____

   _____

3. Who gave the Statue to America? _____

   _____

4. Why did France do it? _____

   _____

5. When did France do it? _____

   _____

F. Grammar check. Use: *me, you, him, her, it, us, them*

1. I like New York. I like *it.*

2. I like Lady Liberty. I like _____.

3. I like New York and Washington, D.C. I like _____.

4. I like Tom. I like _____.

5. I like my friends. I like _____.

6. My teacher teaches Maria and me. She teaches _____.

7. I have a question. Please give _____ the answer.

8. You are very nice. I like _____.

G. Word check. Fill in the blanks.

Use: *tall, beautiful, statues, Liberty, Harbor, symbol, freedom, hope, present.*

1. The Statue of _____ is a symbol of _____.

2. She is in New York _____.

3. She is one of the tallest _____ in the world.

4. She is very _____ and _____.

5. She was a birthday _____ from France.

6. A statue is a _____.

7. She is a symbol of freedom and _____.

H. Listen and write.

1. _____

2. _____

3. _____

4. _____

5. _____

I. Writing check.

Write a postcard to a friend about the Statue of Liberty.

postcard

Vermont

USA 29

1791

J. Pronunciation check.

Lady Liberty   with your torch so high,
shining, shining   in the sky.
We love you 'cause   you are so free,
Lady, Lady   Liberty.
You welcome all   who came to you.
Thank you, thank you   for all you do!

K. Talk about New York and the Statue of Liberty.

Why do people like to visit the Statue of Liberty?
Would you like to visit New York?
What would you like to see?

L. Let's check up on Igor!

(rrrrring)

Laura: Hello?

Igor: Hi, Laura.

Laura: Igor! Where are you?

Igor: I'm still in New York, but I'm leaving.

Laura: Oh no! Where are you going? Boston?

Igor: Paris.

Laura: Paris! France?

Igor: Yeah. Paree!

Laura: But ...

Igor: We're boarding the plane. See you later.

        (Click)

M. Check the internet: < www.nps.gov/stli>

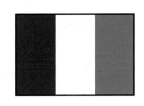

2

Greetings from Paris

PHOTOGRAPHER: © PONTUS EDENBERG | AGENCY: DREAMSTIME.COM

WHAT? the Eiffel Tower   **WHERE? Paris, France**

WHEN? 1889   **WHO? Alexandre Eiffel**

WHY? the World's Fair

A. Where's Igor?

(rrring)

Igor: Hello!

You: Hello, Igor. Now where are you?

Igor: I'm in Paris, France!

You: Ah! I love Paris! Do you like Paris?

Igor: Oh, yes, especially the Eiffel Tower.

You: Really? Are you at the Tower?

Igor: I'm in it! And I can see all of Paris from here!

You: Well, have fun!

Igor: Au revoir!

B. Do you know these words?

a tower _____

a structure _____

famous _____

to climb _____

the top _____

wonderful _____

a view _____

to build _____

a fair _____

Where in the World...

C. Read.

The Eiffel Tower is a tall, beautiful structure in Paris. It is very famous. It is the symbol of Paris. You can climb to the top. You can see all of the beautiful city of Paris. It is a wonderful view. The Eiffel Tower was built for the World's Fair. It was built in 1889 by Alexandre Gustave Eiffel. (59)

D. Answer: *Yes, it is/was.* **or** *No, it isn't/wasn't.*

1. The Eiffel Tower is a house. *No, it isn't.*

2. The Eiffel Tower is in America. _____

3. The Eiffel Tower is very tall. _____

4. It was built in 1789. _____

5. It is a beautiful tower. _____

6. It was built by Alexandre Eiffel. _____

7. It is a symbol for America. _____

8. It was built for the World's Fair. _____

E. Write the answers.

1. What is the Eiffel Tower? _____

_____

2. Where is the Eiffel Tower? _____

3. Who built it? _____

4. When was it built? _____

5. Why was it built? _____

_____

The Eiffel Tower

F. Grammar check. Use *want* or *wants*

1. I _____ to go to Paris.

2. My friend _____ to go with me.

3. My sister _____ to see the Eiffel tower.

4. We _____ to see other places, too.

5. I _____ to practice my French in France.

6. John and Mary _____ to go by plane.

7. They _____ to eat French food.

8. Mary _____ to buy some souvenirs.

9. In France she _____ to travel by train.

G. Word check. Fill in the blanks with these words: *tower, structure, famous, climb, top, wonderful, view, built, Fair*

1. The Eiffel Tower is a beautiful _____.

2. It was built for the World's _____.

3. It was _____ by Alexandre Eiffel.

4. It is very _____.

5. It has a _____ _____ from the top.

6. Can you _____ to the _____?

7. It is a very tall _____.

H. Listen and write.

1. _____

2. _____

3. _____

4. _____

5. _____

Where in the World...

I. Writing check.

Write a postcard to a friend about the Eiffel Tower.

postcard

J. Pronunciation check.

What do you think	when you think of Paris?
What do you see	when you go to Paris?
The Eiffel Tower!	Of course! Of course!
The Eiffel Tower	in Paris, France.

K. Talk about Paris and the Eiffel Tower.

Would you like to go Paris? Why?
Where else in France? Why?
Do you know another famous tower or building?
Where is it? Why is it important?

L. Let's check up on Igor!

(rrrring)

Marie: Allo.

Igor: Marie? It's me, Igor.

Marie: Igor! How are you?

Igor: Fine, Marie. I'm calling to say goodbye.

Marie: No! Why are you leaving? Paris is beautiful in the spring.

Igor: Ah, yes. I love Paris in the springtime. But I also love
         Rome.

Marie: Rome? But ...

Igor: I leave tomorrow. Au revoir.

Marie: Oh, Igor, can't you stay?

Igor: Sorry, I can't. Adieu.

M. Check the internet: <en.wikipedia.org/wiki/Eiffel_Tower>

Saint Peter's Church
Vatican City, Rome, Italy

3

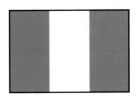

The Vatican

WHAT? Saint Peter's Church

WHERE? Vatican City

WHEN? about 325 C.E.*

WHO? Michelangelo

HOW MANY? 50,000 people

* Common Era. It is the same as A.D. (anno Domini)

A. Where's Igor?

(rrrrring)

You: Hello!

Igor: Hello! Is that you?

You: Yeah, it's me. Where in the world are you?

Igor: I'm in Saint Peter's Church in Italy.

You: Really? You're inside?

Igor: Yeah. It's really quiet here.

You: What's it like?

Igor: Awesome!

You: That's what everybody says.

Igor: Uh oh! I can't use my cell phone in here. Bye.

B. Do you know these words?

a church _____

to hold _____

an architect _____

an artist _____

to design _____

a dome _____

paintings _____

C. Read.

Saint Peter's is the largest Christian church in the world. It can hold over 50,000 people. It is in Vatican City, in Rome. The church was begun a long time ago, about 325 C.E. Through the years, many architects worked on the building. Michelangelo, a famous artist, designed a part of the dome. The church also has beautiful paintings. (59)

D. Answer: *I agree.* **or** *I don't agree.*

1. St. Peter's is a government building. _____

2. St. Peter's dome is beautiful. _____

3. The church can hold 5,000 people. _____

4. Michelangelo was a king. _____

5. St. Peter's is the largest church in the world. _____

6. There are no paintings in the church. _____

7. Vatican City is in Rome. _____

E. Write the answers.

1. What is St. Peter's? _____

2. Where is it? _____

3. Who designed the dome? _____

4. How many people can it hold? _____

5. When was St. Peter's begun? _____

F. Grammar check.

Use the possessive -'s form. Example: *the top of the tower > the tower's top*

1. the church of St. Peter _____

2. the dome of Michelangelo _____

3. the famous places of Rome _____

4. the postcard from a friend _____

5. the churches of Italy _____

6. the work of an artist _____

7. the architect of the building _____

8. the designer of the statue _____

G. Word check.

Fill in the blanks. Use: *church, holds, architect, artists, designed, dome, paintings*

1. Michelangelo _____ the famous dome.

2. St. Peter's _____ 50,000 people.

3. St. Peter's has a beautiful _____.

4. An _____ designs buildings.

5. Many _____ painted many _____.

6. St. Peter's is a _____.

H. Listen and write.

1. _____

2. _____

3. _____

4. _____

5. _____

Where in the World...

I. Writing check.

Write a postcard to a friend about St. Peter's Church.

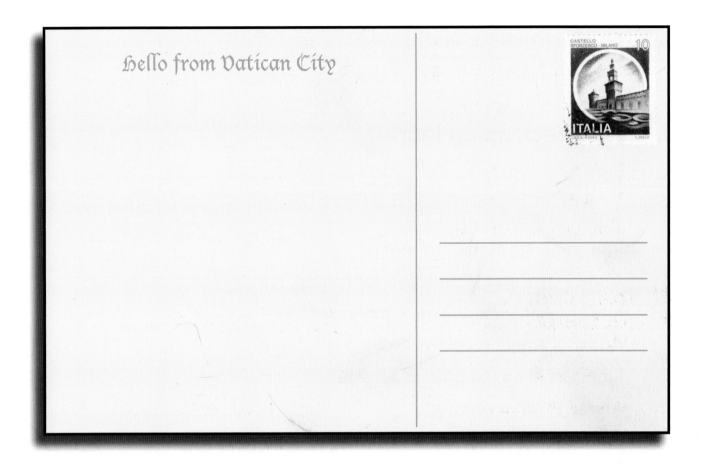

Hello from Vatican City

CASTELLO SFORZESCO · MILANO 10
ITALIA

J. Pronunciation check.

A special trip,	a special trip.
Let's all take	a special trip.
Go to Rome.	See St. Peter's.
Go to Rome.	See St. Peter's.
See the dome	of St. Peter's.
Michelangelo's	famous dome.
When in Rome,	see the dome.
When in Rome,	see the dome.

K. Talk about Rome and St. Peter's.

Would you like to visit St. Peter's? Why?
What about Rome?
Do you know about another "religious" city?
What is it? Do people visit it?

L. Let's check up on Igor.

(rrrrring)

Anna: Hello?

Igor: Anna Maria, it's Igor.

Anna: Oh, Igor. Thank you for calling, I ...

Igor: Anna Maria, I have bad news.

Anna: What do you mean?

Igor: I'm on the train to Athens.

Anna: You're kidding!

Igor: No, really. I went to Venice and ...

Anna: But Igor – our dinner at Bertolini's ...

Igor: I know. Maybe later.

Anna: But Athens? When will you ...

Igor: Anna Maria, it was so good to see you, but now
       – arrivederci, Roma.

M. Check the Internet: <en.wikipedia.org/wiki/Vatican_City>

The Parthenon
Athens, Greece

4

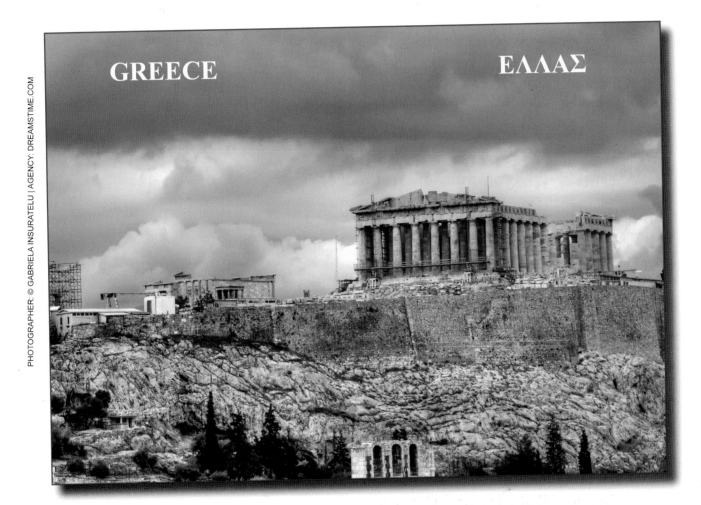

GREECE   ΕΛΛΑΣ

PHOTOGRAPHER: © GABRIELA INSURATELU | AGENCY: DREAMSTIME.COM

WHAT? a temple   **WHERE? Greece**

WHEN? 447– 442 B.C.E.*   **WHO? Athenians, Greeks**

WHY? to guard Athens

* Before the Common Era. It is the same as B.C. (before Christ)

A. Where's Igor?

Igor: Hello!

You: Hello, Igor? Where are you?

Igor: I'm in Greece.

You: In Greece? What are you doing there?

Igor: I'm looking at a famous Greek temple.

You: Where is it?

Igor: It's on a hill called the Acropolis.

You: Oh, you must be at the Parthenon. It must be exciting!

Igor: Very exciting! It's a beautiful place. And my guide is teaching me Greek.

You: Wonderful! What's his name?

Igor: Her name is Eleni.

You: Oh, I see. Well, have fun!

Igor: We will. Thanks for calling. Goodbye.

B. Do you know these words?

a temple _____

between _____

high _____

a hill _____

to honor _____

to guard _____

to protect _____

enemies _____

ruins _____

C. Read.

The Parthenon is a Greek Temple. It is in Athens, Greece. The Parthenon was built between 447 and 442 B.C.E. It is high on a hill, the Acropolis. The Athenians built this temple to honor Athena. The city of Athens is named after her. She was the Goddess of Athens. Athena guarded the city and protected it from enemies. There are many ruins of old cities and temples in Greece. (71)

D. Answer: *That's right.* **or** *That's wrong.*

1. The Parthenon is a building. _____

2. The Parthenon is in Greece. _____

3. The Parthenon is a temple for a king. _____

4. Greece is in Athens. _____

5. There are many ruins in Greece. _____

6. The Acropolis is not on a hill. _____

7. The Parthenon is on the Acropolis. _____

8. Athena honored the Greeks. _____

E. Write the answers.

1. What is the Parthenon? _____

2. Where is it? _____

3. Who is it for? _____

4. Why was it built? _____

5. When was it built? _____

F. Grammar check. Write past tense sentences.

Example: *I want to go. > I wanted to go.*

1. The Greeks love Athena. _____

2. The Greeks honor Athena. _____

3. Athena guards the city. _____

4. She protects the city. _____

5. We look at the Temple. _____

6. They climb the hill. _____

7. We ask many questions. _____

G. Word check. Fill in the blanks.

Use: *temple, between, high, hill, honor, guarded, protected, enemies, ruins*

1. The Athenians wanted to _____ Athena.

2. There are many old _____ in Greece.

3. The temple is on a _____ hill.

4. The _____ of Athena is on the Acropolis.

5. It was built _____ 447 and 442 B.C.E.

6. Athena _____ and _____ the city.

7. The Greeks needed protection from their _____.

8. The Acropolis is a _____.

H. Listen and write.

1. _____

2. _____

3. _____

4. _____

5. _____

I. Writing check.

Write a postcard to a friend about the Parthenon.

The Parthenon • Athens, Greece

J. Pronunciation check.

Look out the window!

It's high on a hill.

Do you see it?

Right over there.

No, over there!

Yes, you're right!

Can't wait to land!

What do you see?

The Acropolis?

The Acropolis?

Right over there?

Oh, what a sight!

The Parthenon!

Can't wait to land!

K. Talk about it.

What do you know about Greece?
Would you like to visit Greece?
What would you like to do there?

L. Let's check up on Igor.

(rrrrring)

Igor: Hello?

Eleni: Igor, where have you been?

Igor: Right here in Athens.

Eleni: I couldn't reach you.

Igor: My cell has been off.

Eleni: Anyway, what are you doing tomorrow?

Igor: I'm leaving for Turkey.

Eleni: What? Are you going to Constantinople?

Igor: Eleni, it's been Istanbul for a long time.

Eleni: I know, I know. I'll miss you. Have a good trip.

Igor: Thanks. Bye bye.

Eleni: Kherete.

M. Check the Internet: <en.wikipedia.org/wiki/Greece>

Ayasofya (Hagia Sophia)
Istanbul, Turkey

5

Istanbul   *Türkiye*

PHOTOGRAPHER: © RAPHAEL HUKAI | AGENCY: DREAMSTIME.COM

WHAT? cathedral, mosque, museum   **WHERE?** Turkey

WHEN? 4th century C.E.   **WHO?** Atatürk

WHY? earthquakes

Ayasofya

A. Where's Igor?

(rrrrring)

Igor: Hello!

You: Hello, Igor? Where are you? Are you still in Athens?

Igor: No, I'm in Turkey.

You: In Turkey? You really get around! Why Turkey?

Igor: I'm visiting the world's great, old places.

You: Like?

Igor: Like Ayasofya.

You: That was the Hagia Sophia, wasn't it?

Igor: Yes, it was. It's a very famous museum now!

You: Send me a postcard.

Igor: I will.

B. Do you know these words?

an earthquake _____

a fire _____

to damage _____

a cathedral _____

a century _____

a mosque _____

a museum _____

gold _____

mosaics _____

C. Read.

Ayasofya is a very old building. It was built and rebuilt many times because earthquakes and fires damaged it. First, it was Hagia Sophia, a cathedral. It was built in the sixth century. Then, it was a mosque. Finally, President Atatürk made it a museum in 1934. It has a beautiful dome. Visitors can look at the beautiful gold mosaics. They are on the floor, on the walls, and on the ceiling. (72)

D. Answer: *Yes, that's correct.* **or** *No, that's incorrect.*

1. Today Ayasofya is a church. _____

2. Today Ayasofya is a museum. _____

3. It was a mosque. _____

4. Ayasofya is in Istanbul. _____

5. It has silver mosaics. _____

6. It has a beautiful dome. _____

7. Earthquakes did not damage it. _____

8. Atatürk made it a mosque. _____

E. Write the answers.

1. What is Ayasofya? _____

2. Where is it? _____

3. Why was it rebuilt? _____

4. When was it made into museum? _____

5. Who made it a museum? _____

F. Grammar check. Change the sentences to negative.

Example: *Atatürk built Ayasofya. (build) > Atatürk did not build Ayasofya.*

1. We went to Iran. (go) _____

2. She saw Romania. (see) _____

3. I bought postcards. (buy) _____

4. He took many pictures. (take) _____

5. I ate Greek food. (eat) _____

6. You slept well on the plane. (sleep) _____

7. They spent a lot of money. (spend) _____

G. Word check. Fill in the blanks.

Use: *Earthquakes, fire, damaged, cathedral, century, mosque, museum, gold, mosaics*

1. Ayasofya was _____ and rebuilt.

2. It was built in the fourth _____ .

3. Today Ayasofya is a _____ .

4. It is decorated with beautiful _____ .

5. _____ and _____ can damage buildings.

6. The mosaics are made with _____ .

7. At first it was a Christian _____ .

8. Then, it was a _____ .

H. Listen and write.

1. _____

2. _____

3. _____

4. _____

5. _____

Where in the World...

I. Writing check.

Write a postcard to a friend about Ayasofya.

Ayasofya   Istanbul

POSTA
TÜRKIYE CUMHURIYETI
70 YENI KURUŞ

_____

_____

_____

_____

J. Pronunciation check.

Turkey!
Turkey!
Half in Asia,
Let's go to see
Ayasofya.
the very same name
a great, great mosque
in Istanbul!

Half in Asia.
Half in Europe.
half in Europe.
Hagia Sophia.
They're the same,
of a great cathedral,
and now a museum
In Istanbul!

K. Talk about it.

Would you like to visit Ayasofya? Why?
What other museums have you visited?
What was the best one? What was special about it?

L. Let's check up on Igor.

(rrrrring)

Clerk:	Alo, Otel Bosfor.
Nermin:	I'm calling for Igor in Room 210.
Clerk:	One moment, please.
Igor:	Hello?
Nermin:	Hi, Igor. Have you got our tickets?
Igor:	I have. Have you got your visas?
Nermin:	All set and ready to go.
Igor:	OK! See you at Atatürk International Airport.
Nermin:	Görüshürüz.

M. Check the Internet: <www.virtualistanbul.com>

PHOTOGRAPHER: © MOSTAFA MOFTAH | AGENCY: DREAMSTIME.COM

Hello from Giza, Egypt

WHAT? the Great Sphinx, a statue

WHERE? Egypt

WHEN? 2,500 B.C.E.

WHO? workers

WHY? Who knows?

HOW BIG? huge

A. Where's Igor?

(rrrrring)

Igor: Hello!

You: Hello! Igor? Where are you?

Igor: I'm in Egypt.

You: What are you doing there?

Igor: Right now, I'm riding a camel.

You: Really? A camel?

Igor: Yes, and I'm looking at the Great Sphinx.

You: Big, isn't it?

Igor: Oh, yeah! Really huge!

You: Well, have a good day.

Igor: You, too. Bye bye.

B. Do you know these words?

body _____

lion _____

king _____

long _____

huge _____

ancient _____

worker _____

pyramid _____

behind _____

Where in the World...

C. Read.

The Great Sphinx is a statue in Egypt. It has the body of a lion and the head of a person, maybe a king. It is huge. It is about 200 feet long and 70 feet high. It's the largest statue from ancient times. It was built about 2,500 B.C.E. Thousands of workers built it. Nobody knows why it was built. There are three great pyramids behind it. Maybe the Great Sphinx is there to guard the pyramids. (79)

D. Answer. Write *true* or *false*.

1. The Great Sphinx is a mountain. *False*

2. It is in Egypt. _____

3. It has the body of a dog. _____

4. It is behind the pyramids. _____

5. Everybody knows why it was made. _____

6. It is not the largest ancient statue. _____

7. The Great Sphinx was built 250 years ago. _____

E. Write the answers.

1. What is the Great Sphinx? _____

2. Where is the Great Sphinx? _____

3. Who built it? _____

4. When was it built? _____

5. Why was it made? _____

F. Grammar check. Use *have* or *has* in the sentences below.

1. Egypt _____ many ancient pyramids.

2. The Great Sphinx _____ the head of a person.

3. It _____ the body of a lion.

4. All countries _____ statues.

5. Some museums _____ statues.

6. Egypt _____ huge statues.

7. Pyramids _____ a special shape.

8. Do you _____ a camera?

G. Word check. Use these words: *lion, king, long, huge, ancient, workers, pyramids, behind*

1. Its body is like a _____.

2. Behind the Sphinx are three _____.

3. It was built in _____ times.

4. The Great Sphinx is a _____ statue.

5. Maybe a _____ built it.

6. It is about 200 feet _____.

7. It was built by _____.

8. The pyramids are _____ the Sphinx.

H. Listen and write.

1. _____

2. _____

3. _____

4. _____

5. _____

Where in the World...

I. Writing check.

Write a postcard to a friend about the Great Sphinx.

Egypt

EGYPT مصر

AIR MAIL

80 P. جوى ق ٨٠ توت عنخ آمون

J. Pronunciation check.

Tell me, tell me
the body of a lion,
A man's head,
A man's head,
It's very very big!
Why was it made?
Nobody knows
Nobody knows.

about the Sphinx,
the head of a man.
a lion's body.
a lion's body.
It's big, it's huge!
Nobody knows.
why it was made.
Nobody. Nobody!

K. Talk about it in small groups.

Would you like to go to Egypt? Why?
What would you like to see?
What famous statues do you know about?
Where are they?

L. Let's check up on Igor.

(rrrrring)

Igor: Hello, this is Igor.

Abdul: Salaam, Igor.

Igor: Abdul, good to hear from you.

Abdul: So, Igor, when did you get here?

Igor: We got here two days ago.

Abdul: We? Who's with you?

Igor: A friend from Istanbul.

Abdul: That's nice. Can I invite you to dinner?

Igor: Abdul, I'm really very sorry. We're leaving this afternoon.

Abdul: Oh, no. So soon?

Igor: Yeah, we've got plane reservations for Dar es Salaam.

Abdul: Tanzania?

Igor: Uh, oh. The taxi's here. Bye, Abdul. See you another time.

Abdul: OK. Safe journey.

M. Check the Internet: <www.touregypt.net/sphinx.htm>

Ngorongoro Game Preserve
Tanzania, Africa

7

WISH YOU WERE HERE

PHOTOGRAPHER: © ALAN WARD | AGENCY: DREAMSTIME.COM

WHAT? safari, crater, game preserve   **WHERE?** Tanzania

WHO? tourists   **WHY?** to see animals

WHAT? bones, early man   **WHEN?** 1999

HOW OLD? 3.5 million years   **WHO?** Meave Leakey

A. Where's Igor?

(rrrrring)

Igor: Hujambo.

You: Where are you?

Igor: In Africa!

You: In Africa! What are you doing there?

Igor: We're on a safari.

You: A safari?

Igor: Yes, we're looking at wild animals, like elephants and lions.

You: Taking a lot of pictures?

Igor: Lots of pictures.

You: Cool! Will you send me some?

Igor: Sure thing! Uh oh ... why is that lion walking toward us? I think ...

You: Igor? Igor! What's going on?

B. Do you know these words?

wildlife _____

park _____

crater _____

volcano _____

safari _____

bones _____

early man _____

anthropologist _____

C. Read.

Ngorongoro Game Preserve is a wildlife park in Tanzania, Africa. It is a huge crater of an old volcano. Over 30,000 animals come and go in the park. Many tourists come here for a safari. Here they can see lots of wild animals. There are elephants and lions and many others.

In 1999, the bones of early man were found near the preserve. The bones were 3.5 million years old! Meave Leakey, an anthropologist, found them. The bones are now in a museum. (83)

D. Answer: *You bet!* (yes) **or** *No way!* (no).

1. Ngorongoro is a safari. _____

2. It is in Transylvania. _____

3. People go to Ngorongoro to see wildlife. _____

4. People see very few animals. _____

5. Ngorongoro crater is huge. _____

6. Early man lived in 3.5 B.C.E. _____

7. The crater was an old volcano. _____

8. Lions are beautiful. _____

E. Write the answers.

What is Ngorongoro? _____

Where is Ngorongoro? _____

Why do people go on a safari? _____

Who is Meave Leakey? _____

When did she find early man? _____

How old are the bones? _____

F. Grammar check. Use *be going to*. Example: *I am going to take a safari.*

1. We _____ go on a safari.

2. I _____ see many animals.

3. My friend _____ take many pictures.

4. _____ you _____ come with us?

5. Where _____ we _____ stay?

6. What _____ we _____ do?

7. When _____ we _____ go?

8. Who _____ pay for the safari?

G. Word check. Fill in the blanks.

Use: *wildlife, crater, volcano, safari, bones, Early man, anthropologist, found*

1. Let's go on a _____ to see wildlife

2. Ngorongoro is a big _____.

3. It is an old _____.

4. An _____ looks for bones of early man.

5. _____ lived here a long time ago.

6. The _____ are now in a museum.

7. Meave Leakey _____ the bones of early man.

8. Game is another name for _____.

H. Listen and write.

1. _____

2. _____

3. _____

4. _____

5. _____

I. Writing check.

Write a post card to a friend about Ngorongoro.

from a friend at
NGORONGORO GAME PRESERVE,
TANZANIA

1889-1989
CENTENARY OF INTER·PARLIAMENTARY UNION
TANZANIA 80!.
PARLIAMENT
IN SESSION

J. Pronunciation check.

Safari, safari!

Zebras, and lions,

All kinds of animals

So bring your camera

These you must take

An African safari!

and elephants, too.

that are not in a zoo.

and binoculars, too!

to Africa with you!

K. Talk about it in small groups.

What kind of wild animals have you seen?

Where do they live?

Would you like to go on a safari?

L. Let's check up on Igor.

(rrrrring)

Ali: Salaam.

Igor: Salaam, Ali. Guess who?

Ali: Hmmm. I'm not sure. Mike?

Igor: Nope. Igor.

Ali: No way! Where are you?

Igor: Guess.

Ali: Oh, I don't know. Tell me.

Igor: Well, it's a long story, but I'll tell you this afternoon.

Ali: What?

Igor: Can you pick me up at the airport?

Ali: Uh, sure thing. What time?

Igor: Four p.m., flight 225 from Dar es Salaam.

Ali: From Africa? Wow! I'll be there.

Igor: Thanks. See you soon. Bye.

Ali: Bye. (click) Hmmmmmm.

M. Check the Internet: <www.tanzania-web.com/parks/ngorongo.htm>

Petra
Jordan

8

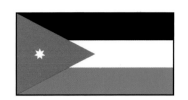

PETRA - ROSE-RED CITY

PHOTOGRAPHER: © HOLGER METTE | AGENCY: DREAMSTIME.COM

WHAT? an ancient city   **WHERE?** Jordan

WHEN? 400 B.C.E. to 500 C.E.   **WHO?** Middle Eastern tribes

WHY? a trading center

A. Where's Igor?

(rrrrring)

Igor: Hello!

You: Hello, Igor? Where the heck are you?

Igor: I'm in Jordan.

You: In Jordan? No kidding! What are you doing there?

Igor: I'm walking around the very, very old city of Petra.

You: Interesting?

Igor: Oh, yes! Interesting and different!

You: Well, I'll let you go.

Igor: Talk to you later.

B . Do you know these words?

a tribe _____

busy _____

to trade _____

a center _____

to buy _____

to sell _____

goods _____

to stand _____

a side _____

a mountain _____

unusual _____

a tomb _____

C. Read.

Petra is an ancient city in Jordan. Different Middle Eastern tribes lived there between 400 B.C.E. and 500 C.E. It was a busy trading center. Traders came to the city on their camels to buy and sell goods. Petra was often called the "Rose-Red City" because the buildings are red in color. Many buildings are still standing. Some are in the side of a mountain. Today, only tourists walk around this unusual city. They come to see the famous temples and tombs. (82)

D. Answer: *I think so, too.* or *I don't think so.*

1. Petra is an important trading center today. _____

2. Petra is in Syria. _____

3. Africans built Petra. _____

4. The temples are red. _____

5. The traders brought goods on camels. _____

6. The temples are on top of a mountain. _____

7. Nobody lives in Petra today. _____

E. Write the answers.

1. What is Petra? _____

2. Where is Petra? _____

3. Who came here? _____

4. Why did they come? _____

5. When was Petra an important trading center? _____

6. Who lived there? _____

F. Grammar check. Write *what, where, who, when, why* for the underlined words.

1. <u>Petra</u> was an important trading center. *what*

2. It is <u>in Jordan</u>. _____

3. <u>Traders</u> came <u>here</u>. _____ _____

4. It was a busy place <u>in 400 B.C.E.</u> _____

5. Is it a trading center <u>today</u>? _____

6. Is it an <u>ancient city</u>? _____

7. It is called the Rose-Red City <u>because</u> of the red stone. _____

8. <u>People</u> lived <u>there</u>. _____ _____

G. Word check. Fill in the blanks: *tribes, busy, traders, center, buy, sell, goods, side, mountain, unusual, tombs*

1. People who buy and sell are _____.

2. Many Middle Eastern _____ lived there.

3. It was a very _____ city with a lot of buying and selling.

4. The traders came to _____ and _____ things.

5. The temples are built into the _____ of a _____.

6. It is an _____ city.

7. The traders came to the trading _____ with their _____.

8. Tourists come to see the temples and _____.

H. Listen and write.

1. _____

2. _____

3. _____

4. _____

5. _____

I. Writing check.

Write a postcard to a friend about Petra.

```
POSTCARD                          [stamp]
                                  POSTAGE  1999
                                  AL - Hussein Tournament
                                  100 FILS  H.K. OF JORDAN



                          _____

                          _____

                          _____

                          _____


PETRA: THE HASHEMITE KINGDOM OF JORDAN
```

J. Pronunciation check.

Go back in time   to a long time ago,
long, long ago   to a place once busy,
buying and selling   buying and selling.
To a city of stone,   of red, red stone,
beautiful, beautiful   red, red stone.
Go to Petra!   Go and see
the famous city,   the Rose-Red City!

K. Talk about Petra.

Would you like to visit Petra?
What do you know about the Middle East?
What would you see there?
Would you like to ride a camel?

L. Let's check up on Igor.

Ali:	Salaam.
Igor:	Salaam, Ali, It's me again. I'm calling from Petra.
Ali:	Igor, what's up?
Igor:	Well, can I ask a favor?
Ali:	I guess so. What is it?
Igor:	Can you meet me at the bus station at two?
Ali:	Yeah, I guess so. Why?
Igor:	I have to get to the airport by four.
Ali:	You mean you can't stay tonight?
Igor:	No. I've got to get to Moscow. I have to ...
Ali:	Igor? Are you there? I can't hear you. Can you hear me? Can you hear me? ... Cut off!

M. Check the Internet:
<www.brown.edu/Departments/Anthropology/Petra>

Where in the World...

St. Basil's Cathedral
Moscow, Russia

9

WHAT? a cathedral

WHO? Ivan the Terrible

WHEN? 1555-1560

WHERE? Red Square, Moscow, Russia

WHY? to celebrate a victory

St. Basil's Cathedral

PHOTOGRAPHER: © ELENA ELISSEEVA | AGENCY: DREAMSTIME.COM

A. Where's Igor?

(rrrrring)

Igor: Hello.

You: Hello, Igor? How are things in Jordan?

Igor: I'm not in Jordan. I'm in Moscow.

You: In Russia? Why are you in Russia?

Igor: I'm meeting some old friends in Red Square.

You: Who?

Igor: You don't know them. They're waiting for me at St. Basil's Cathedral.

You: Tell me more!

Igor: I'll tell you later. I've got to go.

B. Do you know these words?

to celebrate _____

a victory _____

a czar _____

insane _____

terrible _____

to kill _____

including _____

historical _____

C. Read.

St. Basil's is an unusual cathedral with many domes and towers. It was built between 1555 and 1560. Ivan IV built it to celebrate a victory. He was a czar, and he was also insane. He was called Ivan the Terrible because he killed many people, including his son. The Cathedral is in Red Square in Moscow. There are many other historical places in and around Red Square, including the Kremlin, the center of the Russian government. Today many people visit these places. (83)

D. Answer: *Yes, that's true.* **or** *No, that isn't true.*

1. Is St. Basil's a cathedral? _____

2. Is St. Basil's in the Kremlin? _____

3. Was the Cathedral built in 1914? _____

4. Is St. Basil's a mosque? _____

5. Was Ivan IV insane? _____

6. Was he a kind man? _____

7. Did he kill his son? _____

8. Did Peter the Great build the cathedral? _____

E. Write the answer.

1. What is St. Basil's? _____

2. Where is it? _____

3. Who built it? _____

4. Why did he build it? _____

5. When did he build it? _____

F. Grammar check. Complete the word.

Example: *Did they sell their goods?*

1. I live in m_____ city.

2. You damaged y_____r car.

3. She protects h_____r children.

4. Did he kill h_____s own people?

5. We celebrated o_____r victory.

6. Marie and Mike work in t_____r store.

7. Do you and Marie work in y_____r store every day?

G. Word check.

Fill in the blanks with *celebrated, victory, czar, insane, Terrible, killed, including, historical*

1. Red Square has many _____ places, _____ the Kremlin.

2. They _____ a great victory.

3. He was crazy; he was an _____ person.

4. Ivan IV was Ivan the _____.

5. Ivan IV _____ many people.

6. He was a Russian _____.

7. After the _____ everybody celebrated.

H. Listen and write.

1. _____

2. _____

3. _____

4. _____

5. _____

I. Writing check.

Write a postcard to a friend about Russia.

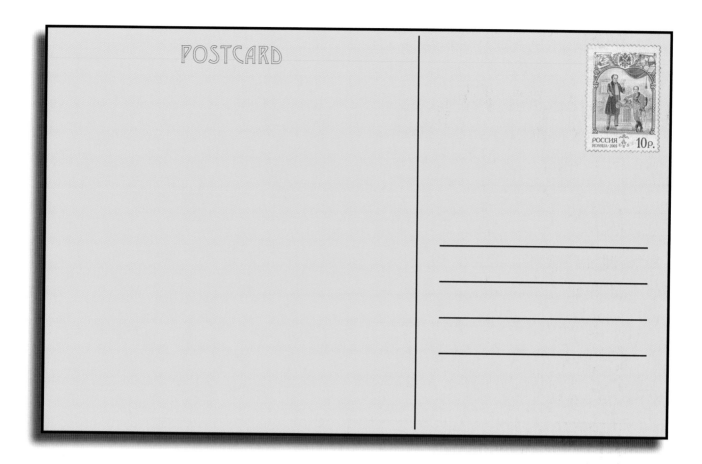

POSTCARD

РОССИЯ
ROSSIA·2003 10р.

J. Pronunciation check.

Who was Ivan,
Ivan the IV.
Aha! A czar,
Was he bad?
Really, really bad?
What was he called?
Terrible Ivan?
A terrible czar?

Ivan the IV?
A czar, a czar!
a Russian czar!
Yes, he was bad.
Really, really bad!
Terrible, Terrible.
Ivan the Terrible.
A terrible czar.

St. Basil's Cathedral

K. Talk about it in small groups.

Do you know of other terrible rulers like Ivan the Terrible?
Where did they live? What did they do?
Who were some good rulers?

L. Let's check up on Igor.

(rrrrring)

Olga: Hello.

Manju: Hello? I'm calling for Igor.

Olga: Who's this?

Manju: It's Manju, a friend of Igor.

Olga: Where are you calling from?

Manju: Delhi. I'm expecting Igor.

Olga: Delhi's in India, isn't it?

Manju: Yes, but can I speak with Igor?

Olga: He isn't here.

Manju: Where is he?

Olga: I don't know! Do svidanya.

M. Check the Internet: <www.geographia.com/russia/moscow03.htm>

10

PHOTOGRAPHER: © XDREW | AGENCY: DREAMSTIME.COM

Evening at
the Taj Mahal

WHAT? the Taj Mahal, a tomb, a memorial

WHERE? Agra, India

WHEN? 1632-1653

WHO? Shah Jahan

WHY? to remember his wife, Mumtaz Mahal

A. Where's Igor?

(rrrrring)

Igor: Hello!

You: Is that you, Igor? Where are you now? Bulgaria?

Igor: I'm in India.

You: No way! In India? What are you doing there?

Igor: I'm visiting the Taj Mahal.

You: What's the Taj Mahal?

Igor: It's a very, very famous tomb.

You: Really? Whose tomb?

Igor: The tomb of a Shah's wife!

You: Well, I just wanted to catch up with you. Gotta run!

Igor: Stay in touch.

B. Do you know these words?

incredible _____

a river _____

an emperor _____

a memorial _____

to die _____

to remember _____

forever _____

marble _____

gems _____

a garden _____

C. Read.

The Taj Mahal is an incredibly beautiful tomb on the Jumna River in the city of Agra. It was built a long time ago (1632-1653) by the Emperor of India, Shah Jahan. It is a memorial for his wife, Mumtaz Mahal. The Shah loved her very much. When she died he wanted to remember her forever, so he built the Taj Mahal. It is made of white marble. You can see many gems on the floor and walls. There are beautiful gardens there, too. Many people come to see it. (90)

D. Answer: *Yes, you're right about that.* **or** *No, you're wrong about that.*

1. The Taj Mahal is a tomb. _____

2. It's in Iran. _____

3. It was built for the emperor. _____

4. I think it was built for Shah Jahan. _____

5. Mumtaz Mahal was his son. _____

6. I believe he loved his wife very much. _____

7. It's near a river. _____

8. It's in the city of Agra. _____

E. Write the answers. Then practice with a classmate.

What's the Taj Mahal? _____

Where's the Taj Mahal? _____

Who built it? _____

When was it built? _____

Why was it built? _____

The Taj Mahal

F. Grammar check. Use past tense verbs in the exercises.

1. Did you go by plane? Yes, _I went by plane._

2. Did you see the Taj Mahal? Yes, _____

3. Did you have a guide? Yes, _____

4. Did you take pictures? Yes, _____

5. Did you visit friends? Yes, _____

6. Did you look at the gardens? Yes, _____

7. Did you eat Indian food? Yes, _____

8. Did you sleep in a hotel? Yes, _____

G. Word check. Fill in the blanks.

Use: *incredible, River, emperor, memorial, died, remember, forever, marble, gardens*

1. The _____ outside the building are beautiful.

2. The Shah was the _____ of India.

3. He built the Taj Mahal to _____ his wife.

4. She was young when she _____.

5. He wanted to remember her _____.

6. The Taj Mahal is a _____ on the Jumna _____.

7. I can't believe it; it's _____.

8. The tomb is made of _____.

H. Listen and write.

1. _____

2. _____

3. _____

4. _____

5. _____

I. Writing check.

Write a postcard to a friend about the Taj Mahal.

postcard

भारत INDIA
10.00
TIGER · SUNDARBANS BIOSPHERE RESERVE

_____

_____

_____

_____

J. Pronunciation check.

The Shah of India was very sad
when his wife passed away.
So sad was he that he built a tomb
for his wife who died. She passed away;
yes, passed away, but her memory stays
at the Taj Mahal, at the Taj Mahal.

K. Talk about it in small groups.

What other tombs do you know about?
Who is buried there? Why is this person famous?
Where is this tomb?

L. Let's check up on Igor.

(rrrrring)

Igor: Namaste.

Manju: Namaste, Igor. You're back. Wasn't the Taj incredible?

Igor: Beautiful, incredible!

Manju: And it was built because of a love between a man and a woman.

Igor: Yes, that's incredible.

Manju: What do you mean?

Igor: I just mean he really liked his wife.

Manju: Liked? He loved her.

Igor: Oh, yeah. Of course he did. Uh, Manju, have you ever been to Nepal?

Manju: No, why?

Igor: I'm taking the train tomorrow. I want to climb Mount Everest.

Manju: Igor, you are crazy! Goodbye!

Igor: But ...

M. Check the Internet: <www.Greatbuildings.com/buildings/TajMahal.html>

Mount Everest
Nepal and Tibet

11

The Top of the World

PHOTOGRAPHER: © ARTUR MATYSIK | AGENCY: DREAMSTIME.COM

WHAT? Mount Everest

WHERE? Nepal and Tibet

WHO? Sir Edmund Hillary
Tenzing Norgay

WHEN? 1953

WHY? Because it's there

HOW TALL? 8,850 meters

A. Where's Igor?

(rrrrring)

You: Hello.

Igor: Guess where I am now.

You: Let's see. You were in India last week, right?

Igor: Right.

You: Sri Lanka? Bangladesh? Pakistan?

Igor: Guess again.

You: I give up.

Igor: I'm in Nepal.

You: In Nepal? What are you doing there?

Igor: I'm going to climb Mount Everest.

You: You're kidding, aren't you?

Igor: Actually I am, but here comes the bus to the base of the mountain. Bye for now.

B. Do you know these words?

a border _____

dangerous _____

air _____

thin _____

weather _____

a snowstorm _____

to try _____

a guide _____

C. Read.

Mount Everest is the tallest mountain in the world. It is on the border between Nepal and Tibet. Climbing Mount Everest is very dangerous. It is very, very cold. The air is very thin. The weather is terrible. There are big snowstorms. Many people have tried to climb it. Many people have died on Mount Everest. The first men to climb it were Sir Edmund Hillary from New Zealand and his guide, Tenzing Norgay, from Nepal. They did it in 1953. Today many tourists climb Mount Everest. (87)

D. Answer: *That's wrong.* **or** *That's right.*

1. Mount Everest is 8,850 feet high. _____

2. Climbing Mount Everest is dangerous. _____

3. Mount Everest is in India. _____

4. Nobody has died on Mount Everest. _____

5. Hillary reached the top alone. _____

6. The weather on Everest is terrible. _____

7. Three men got to the top in 1953. _____

E. Write the answer.

1. What is Mount Everest? _____

2. Where is Mount Everest? _____

3. Who climbed Mount Everest? _____

4. Why did they climb it? _____

5. When did they climb it? _____

F. Grammar check. Use: *Do* or *Does*.

1. _____ you like to climb a mountain?

2. _____ your guide climb the mountain every year?

3. _____ the students like to climb mountains?

4. _____ children like to climb mountains?

5. _____ you want to go to Tibet?

6. _____ the airplane go to Tibet?

7. _____ it cost a lot of money?

G. Word check. Fill in the blanks.

Use: *border, dangerous, air, thin, weather, snowstorm, try, guide*

1. Climbing Mount Everest is _____.

2. The _____ is terrible, but many people _____ to climb Everest every year.

3. The _____ on Mount Everest is very _____.

4. It's difficult to see in a _____.

5. You have to have a _____ — someone who knows the mountain well.

6. Mount Everest is on the _____ between two countries.

H. Listen and write.

1. _____

2. _____

3. _____

4. _____

5. _____

I. Writing check.

Write a postcard to a friend about Mount Everest.

Mount Everest
8,850 meters

R.1
NEPAL

J. Pronunciation check.

Some want to climb the tallest mountain.

Is that for you? That's not for me!

A pretty big mountain? No, not for me.

And not for me! What about them?

That's not for them! But some want to climb.

What about him? How about her?

A dangerous mountain? That's not for them.

I want to climb. I think we should.

A pretty small mounain? That sounds good.

K. Talk about it in small groups.

Do you like to climb mountains? Why or why not?
Where did you climb? What's the highest mountain you have climbed?

L. Let's check up on Igor.

(rrrrring)

Manju: Hello?

Igor: Manju?

Manju: Igor! Why are you calling?

Igor: Well, I, uh, miss you.

Manju: Sure, you do!

Igor: I do!

Manju: So what do you want now?

Igor: Well, I'm thinking of going to Tibet. Want to come along?

Manju: Are you serious?

Igor: Yeah. It will be really different. The roof of the world.

Manju: It's too cold in the mountains. I'll take the floor — Thai beaches and the sea. So, no thanks.

M. Check the Internet: <www.peakware.com/peaks.html?pk=80>

12

Welcome to Tibet

PHOTOGRAPHER: © DENGYINCHAI | AGENCY: DREAMSTIME.COM

WHAT? a palace, a center   **WHERE? Lhasa, Tibet**

WHO? the Dalai Lama   **WHEN? 7th century**

HOW BIG? over 1,000 rooms

A. Where's Igor?

(rrrrring)

You: Hello.

Igor: Hello, it's me again — your world traveler.

You: Where are you?

Igor: I'm in Lhasa.

You: Lhasa? Where's that?

Igor: Tibet. I'm touring the great Potala Palace.

You: Really? What's it like?

Igor: It's extremely big, and really, really beautiful!

You: What's it like in Tibet?

Igor: Uh, I can't talk right now. I'll tell you later. Bye.

You: Bye.

B. Do you know these words?

a palace _____

religious _____

Buddhists _____

a leader _____

political _____

exile _____

jewels _____

cultural _____

economic _____

C. Read.

The Potala Palace is in Lhasa, Tibet. It is a religious center for Buddhists. It is the home of the Dalai Lama. The Dalai Lama is the leader of Tibetan Buddhists. He is also the political leader. Today, he is in exile in India because Tibet is not a free country. Today, the Palace is a museum. It has over 1,000 rooms. All have beautiful jewels and paintings. The Palace was built a long time ago. It was built in the 7th century. The city of Lhasa is also the cultural and economic center of Tibet. (96)

D. Answer.

For example: Where is Agra? *India.*

1. Where is the Potala Palace? _____

2. What is the palace today? _____

3. How many rooms does the palace have? _____

4. When was the palace built? _____

5. Who is the Dalai Lama? _____

6. Where is the Dalai Lama? _____

7. Who is the leader of Tibet? _____

E. Write the answers.

1. What is Potala Palace? _____

2. Where is Potala Palace? _____

3. Who lives there? _____

4. Why was it built? _____

5. When was it built? _____

F. Grammar check. Use: *was* or *were*

1. I _____ in Tibet.

2. She _____n't in Lhasa.

3. _____ he in Nepal?

4. We _____ in India.

5. _____n't you in Rome?

6. When _____ John and Mary there?

7. When _____ your friend there?

8. Who _____ in Moscow?

G. Word check. Fill in the blanks. Use: *palace, religion, leader, political, exile, jewels, culture, economic*

1. Buddhism is a _____.

2. Music and art are part of a country's _____.

3. Who is the _____ of Tibetan Buddhism?

4. He is in _____ in India.

5. He is also the _____ leader.

6. The Potala is a _____.

7. The rooms have many beautiful _____ .

8. Money and trade are part of the _____ system.

H. Listen and write.

1. _____

2. _____

3. _____

4. _____

5. _____

I. Writing check.

Write a postcard to a friend about Tibet.

```
postcard                                          中国邮政
                                                  CHINA
                                                            1元

                                        _____

                                        _____

                                        _____

                                        _____
```

J. Pronunciation check.

The Potala Palace,	it's in Tibet.
A Buddhist palace	in Tibet.
Come and see	this unusual place.
It's the palace home	of the Dalai Lama,
living in India,	living in exile
from his home	in Tibet.

K. Talk about it in small groups.

Would you like to go to Tibet? Why or why not?
Have you visited a religious center?
Do you know about the history of Tibet?

L. Check up on Igor.

(rrrrring)

Man: Wei?

Igor: Hello, do you speak English?

Man: English? Who is this?

Igor: My name is Igor. I am calling for Wu Jing. Is this the right number?

Man: Yes, it is. I am Wu Jing's father. Who are you?

Igor: I am a friend of Wu Jing. We were students in America.

Man: Ah. I see. Are you in America?

Igor: No. I'm in Tibet.

Man: Tibet? Why are you in Tibet?

Igor: I, uh, am traveling around the world.

Man: I see.

Igor: May I speak with Wu Jing?

Man: She expects your call?

Igor: No. It's a surprise.

Man: I see. I will give her the message. Thank you.

M. Check the Internet: < en.wikipedia.org/wiki/Tibet>

13

ANCIENT XI'AN

WHAT? statues, warriors, a tomb

WHERE? Xi'an China

WHEN? 1974

WHO? Qin Emperor

WHY? to guard the tomb

HOW MANY? more than 7,000

PHOTOGRAPHER: © CJ YU | AGENCY: DREAMSTIME.COM

A. Where's Igor?

(rrrrring)

Igor: Hello!

You: Hello? Igor? Where are you?

Igor: I'm in Xi'an China.

You: In China? I thought you were in Tibet. What are you doing there?

Igor: I'm visiting the Terra Cotta Warriors.

You: Really? Are you at an army base?

Igor: Yes, an ancient army – thousands of statues — all underground!

You: Wow! That's something!

Igor: Well, zaijian!

You: Zaijian? That's goodbye?

Igor: In China, it is. Zaijian.

B. Do you know these words?

a warrior _____

to bake _____

a soldier _____

an army _____

a horse _____

life-size _____

to fight _____

to bury _____

underground _____

C. Read.

The Terra Cotta Warriors are statues. They are made of baked clay. They are statues of soldiers. There are more than 7,000 soldiers – a whole army! There are statues of horses, too. They are all life-size. They are ready to fight! They guard the tomb of an emperor. It is for the First Qin Emperor of China. These statues are in a special tomb. And they were all buried underground. The Terra Cotta Warriors were found in 1974. Today they are a museum in Xi'an, one of the oldest cities in the world. (93)

D. Answer: *Yes, that's true.* or *No, that's false.*

1. The Terra Cotta Warriors are in India. _____

2. The statues are made of clay. _____

3. The Terra Cotta Warriors are emperors. _____

4. There are 700 Warriors. _____

5. They were found in 1794. _____

6. The soldiers guard the emperor. _____

7. The tomb is now a museum. _____

8. Xi'an is a new city. _____

E. Write the answer.

1. What are the Terra Cotta Warriors? _____

2. Where are they? _____

3. Who is buried there? _____

4. Why were the Terra Cotta Warriors made? _____

5. When were they found? _____

F. Grammar check. Write and say the plurals of the following.

Example: *statue > statues*

warrior _____

soldier _____

army _____

emperor _____

city _____

country _____

horse _____

place _____

size _____

person _____

woman _____

man _____

G. Word check. Fill in the blanks.

Use: *Warriors, baked, soldiers, army, horses, life-size, fight, buried, underground*

1. There are over 7,000 Terra Cotta _____.

2. There are statues of _____ and _____.

3. There are many soldiers in an _____.

4. The warriors are ready to _____ for the emperor.

5. They are _____.

6. They are made of _____ clay.

7. It is an _____ museum.

8. When people die, they are _____.

H. Listen and write.

1. _____

2. _____

3. _____

4. _____

5. _____

I. Writing check.

Write a postcard to a friend about the Terra Cotta Warriors.

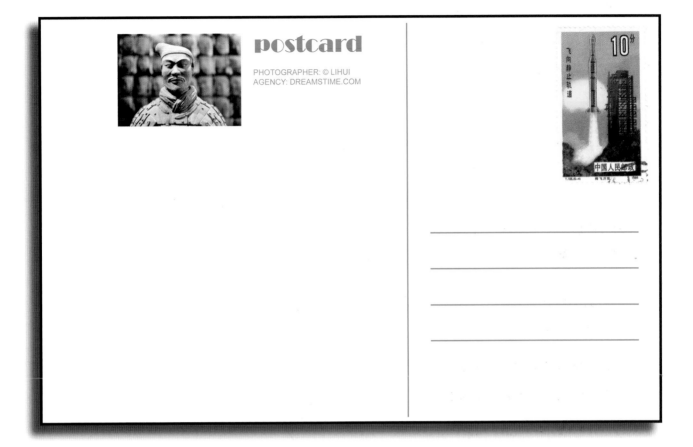

J. Pronunciation check.

Terra cotta,
Soldiers and horses,
What are they like?
Big as life?
Let's go see them.
Big as life?
All in China?
Underground,
Underground!

terra cotta!
horses and soldiers!
Big as life!
And made of clay.
Come and see them.
Big as life!
All underground.
all in China.
Underground!

K. Talk about it.

What do you know about China?
Would you like to go there?
What would you like to do and see?

L. Let's check up on Igor.

(rrrrring)

Wu Jing: Wei?

Igor: Jing?

Wu Jing: Yes. Who's this?

Igor: Igor.

Wu Jing: Really? Igor from America?

Igor: In person, and in China.

Wu Jing: Unbelievable!

Igor: So, are you free this weekend?

Wu Jing: Uh, well, yes! Of course!

Igor: Great! Can you meet me in Jinshanling?

Wu Jing: You're at the Wall? Well, I ... I guess so.

Igor: Good! See you!

M. Check the Internet:

<www.travelchinaguide.com/cityguides/xian/terracotta.htm>

14

PHOTOGRAPHER: © LAMBERT PARREN | AGENCY: DREAMSTIME.COM

WHAT? the Great Wall   **WHERE?** China

WHEN? 200 B.C.E.   **WHO?** workers, tourists

WHY? to protect   **HOW LONG?** 1,500 miles

A. Where's Igor?

Wu Jing: Hello. This is Wu Jing.

You: Sorry, wrong number.

Wu Jing: Wait! This is Igor's phone.

You: Oh! Where's Igor?

Wu Jing: He's on the Wall.

You: What! Wait just a minute. Igor's no gecko.

Wu Jing: No, no! He's walking on the Great Wall.

You: Well, when he gets off the Wall, have him call me.

Wu Jing: OK. What's your number?

You: It's ...

B. Do you know these words?

a wall _____

to wind _____

a province _____

the west _____

the sea _____

the moon _____

a worker _____

to finish _____

a way _____

C. Read.

The Great Wall is in China. It is 1,500 miles long. It winds from Gansu province in the west to the Yellow Sea. It is 25 feet high. It is so big that some say you can see it from space! It took many centuries to build this Wall. Through the years, thousands of Chinese workers built it. It was finished in 200 B.C.E. They built it to keep their enemies out. But the Wall did not protect them. Enemies found ways to climb over the Wall. Today, tourists come to see and walk along the Great Wall. (100)

D. Answer: *Yes, exactly!* or *Sorry, you're wrong.*

1. The Great Wall is in China, isn't it? _____

2. The Great Wall is not very big, is it? _____

3. The Great Wall is 100 feet high, isn't it? _____

4. You can see it from the Eiffel Tower, can't you? _____

5. It was built to keep out enemies, wasn't it? _____

6. It is important for tourism, isn't it? _____

7. The enemies climbed over the Wall, didn't they? _____

8. It took only one century to build, didn't it?_____

E. Write the answers.

1. Where is the Great Wall? _____

2. How long is it? _____

3. Who built it? _____

4. Why did they build it? _____

5. How long did it take to build it? _____

F. Grammar check. Change to questions.

Example: *The Wall is in China. (it) > Is it in China?*

1. I am going to visit China soon. (you) _____

2. He is going to like China. (he)_____

3. We are going to see the Great Wall. (you) _____

4. They are going to go with friends. (they) _____

5. She is going to travel by train. (she)_____

6. John and Mary are going to walk along the Wall. (they)_____

G. Word check. Fill in the blanks.

Use: *winds, Province, west, Sea, space, workers, finish, worked, way, Wall*

1. The Great _____ is very big.

2. It _____ through northern China.

3. It goes from the Yellow _____ to Gansu _____.

4. You can see it from _____.

5. It took centuries to _____ it.

6. Thousands of _____ _____ on it.

7. Taking a tour is the best _____ to see China.

8. East is the opposite of _____.

H. Listen and write.

1. _____

2. _____

3. _____

4. _____

5. _____

I. Writing check.

Write a postcard to a friend about the Great Wall.

J. Pronunciation check.

Imagine a wall
all the way from space,
That's what you see
from space!
a very big wall,
In China,
it built a Great Wall
to keep enemies out,

you can see from space,
from space!
from space,
A very long wall,
in China.
a country so big
to keep enemies out,
but still they came in.

K. Talk about it in small groups.

Was the Great Wall a good idea?
Why or why not?
What do countries build or do for protection?

L. Where's Igor going?

Jing:	**Wei?**
Igor:	**Jing, it's me!**
Jing:	**Where are you now? Shanghai?**
Igor:	**I'm at the airport in Seoul.**
Jing:	**Korea? I thought you were going to Shanghai and then back here.**
Igor:	**I, uh, changed my mind.**
Jing:	**I see. How come?**
Igor:	**I can explain.**
Jing:	**Oh, really?**
Igor:	**Yeah. I had a great time with you at the wall and in Beijing, but I have to be in Tokyo this afternoon and ... Jing? Are you still there? Jing?**

M. Check the Internet: < www.greatwall.org.uk>

Where in the World...

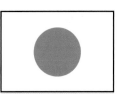

15

PHOTOGRAPHER: © HIROSHI ICHIKAWA | AGENCY: DREAMSTIME.COM

FUJI SAN

WHO? Japanese people   **WHAT?** climb

WHAT? a mountain   **WHERE?** Japan

WHEN? evening   **WHY?** to watch

A. Where's Igor?

(rrrrring)

You: Hello!

Igor: Hi. This ... is Igor.

You: Where are you? Let me guess. Korea?

Igor: No. I'm ... in Japan.

You: What are you doing there?

Igor: I'm hiking ... to the top of Mount Fuji.

You: Really? Can you climb Fuji?

Igor: Yeah ... everybody does.

You: Tell me about it.

Igor: I'd like ... to do ... that ... but I'm almost ... on the top ...
and I'm ... out of breath.

You: OK. I'll let you go. Enjoy!

Igor: Yeah ... this ... is ... really ... fun. ... Bye.

B. Do you know these words?

a cone _____

sacred _____

a trip _____

to stay _____

overnight _____

to watch _____

to come up _____

to breathe _____

fresh _____

Where in the World...

C. Read.

At 12,388 feet, Mount Fuji is the tallest mountain in Japan. It is an old volcano, a perfect cone. Mount Fuji has another name. The Japanese people call it "Fuji san." Mount Fuji is sacred — very special to the Japanese people. They love Mount Fuji and they make special trips to it. They usually visit it in the summer. They like to climb it in the evening. They stay overnight. They breathe the fresh air and watch the sun come up in the morning. This is something the Japanese people love to do. Mount Fuji became a national park in 1936. (100)

D. Answer: *I think that's right.* or *I don't think that's right.*

1. Mount Fuji is a small mountain. _____

2. Mount Fuji is in Tokyo. _____

3. Mount Fuji has a special name. _____

4. Mount Fuji is a new volcano. _____

5. Mount Fuji is a national park. _____

6. People like to go in the winter. _____

7. People like to watch the sunrise. _____

8. People climb in the morning. _____

E. Write the answers.

What is Mount Fuji? _____

Where is Mount Fuji? _____

Who goes to Mount Fuji? _____

When do they go? _____

Why do they go? _____

F. Grammar check. Use: *This* or *These*

1. _____ is Mount Fuji.

2. _____ people are tourists.

3. _____ trip is long.

4. _____ walls are high.

5. _____ colors are not very good.

6. _____ mountain is beautiful.

7. _____ mountains are beautiful.

8. _____ park is nice.

G. Word check. Fill in the blanks.

Use: *cone, sacred, trip, stay, overnight, watch, come up, breathe, fresh*

1. People _____ overnight.

2. They take a _____ to the mountain.

3. They _____ the fresh air.

4. They _____ the beautiful sunrise.

5. Fuji is a _____ mountain for the Japanese.

6. They stay _____ to watch the sun _____.

7. It's great to breathe the _____ air.

8. Mount Fuji is shaped like a _____.

H. Listen and write.

1. _____

2. _____

3. _____

4. _____

5. _____

I. Writing check.

Write a postcard to a friend about Mount Fuji.

POSTCARD

NIPPON 80

J. Pronunciation check.

Mount Fuji,
Japan,
It's a beautiful mountain.
A beautiful mountain.
Japan, Japan.
to Japan,

Mount Fuji,
Japan!
What did you say?
Where did you say?
Let's all of us go
to Japan!

K. Talk about it.

Why is Mount Fuji special?
Do you know any sacred places? Where?
Why do people go there?

L. It's Igor!

(rrrrring)

Kenji: Mushi, mushi.

Igor: Kenji san. It's Igor!

Kenji: Hey, Igor san. It was a great weekend, wasn't it?

Igor: Fantastic! Sunrise on Fuji was unforgettable.

Kenji: It was. And my sister really enjoyed meeting you.

Igor: She did?

Kenji: Yeah. She's hoping you'll stay over a little longer.

Igor: Oh, that would be nice, but my plane leaves tomorrow.

Kenji: Ah! Too bad. So where are you going tomorrow?

Igor: Kampuchea.

Kenji: It should be interesting. Sayonara, Igor.

Igor: Sayonara. Say hello to Mariko.

Kenji: OK. Sayonara.

M. Check the Internet: <www.japan-guide.com/e/e6901.html>

Angkor Wat
Cambodia/Kampuchea

16

PHOTOGRAPHER: © RENARD VARDY | AGENCY: DREAMSTIME.COM

The Jungle Temple
Angkor Wat

WHAT? a temple   **WHERE? Cambodia/Kampuchea**

WHEN? 1100s   **WHO? Hindus, Buddhists**

Angkor Wat   **91**

A. Where's Igor?

(rrrrring)

Igor: Hello!

You: Hello, Igor? Where are you?

Igor: I'm at a wat.

You: You're at a what?

Igor: A wat—actually Angkor Wat—a temple in Kampuchea.

You: You're at Camp Uchea?

Igor: No, no, not a camp. I'm in Cambodia, also known as Kampuchea.

You: Oh! Cambodia in Southeast Asia.

Igor: Right. I'm going in the temple now. So long for now.

You: Call me back later. Bye bye.

B. Do you know these words?

a capital _____

a kingdom _____

Hindus _____

stone _____

to carve _____

a story _____

history _____

a flag _____

proud _____

C. Read.

Angkor was the capital city of the Khmer kingdom in Southeast Asia many years ago. It was a religious center for Hindus and Buddhists. Angkor has many temples. The temples have many wonderful stone carvings. The carvings tell many stories about the history of the Cambodian people. Every year, more and more ancient buildings are found in Angkor. Angkor Wat is an unusually large temple in Cambodia. Angkor means capital. Wat means temple. It was built in the 1100s. Look at the flag of Cambodia. There is a picture of Angkor Wat on the flag. The people of Cambodia are very proud of Angkor Wat. (105)

D. Answer: *Yes, in fact, it is.* or *Actually, it isn't.*

Example: Is Kampuchea also Cambodia? *Yes, in fact, it is.*

1. Is Angkor Wat in Cambodia? _____

2. Is Angkor Wat on the flag of Vietnam? _____

3. Is Angkor Wat a new city? _____

4. Is Angkor Wat a temple? _____

5. Is Angkor Wat very unusual? _____

6. Is Angkor Wat the capital now? _____

7. Is Angkor Wat small? _____

E. Write the answers.

1. What is Angkor Wat? _____

2. Where is Angkor Wat? _____

3. When was it built? _____

4. What is Angkor? _____

5. Who is proud of Angkor Wat? _____

F. Grammar check. Write questions with *isn't it?* or *wasn't it?*

Example: *It is large, > It is large, isn't it ?*

1. Angkor Wat is large, _____?

2. It is a temple, _____?

3. It was a capital city, _____?

4. It's on the flag, _____?

5. It was built in the 1100s, _____?

6. It's unusual, _____?

7. It was in the Khmer Kingdom, _____?

G. Word check. Use: *capital, kingdom, Hindu, stone, carvings, stories, history, flag, proud*

1. Angkor was a _____ and Buddhist center.

2. A picture of Angkor Wat is on the _____ of Cambodia.

3. Angkor was the capital of the Khmer _____.

4. The Cambodian people are _____ of Angkor Wat.

5. The temples have many _____ carvings.

6. Angkor was the _____ city many years ago.

7. Angkor Wat has beautiful stone _____ on the walls.

8. The carvings tell many _____ about the _____ of Cambodia.

H. Listen and write.

1. _____

2. _____

3. _____

4. _____

5. _____

Where in the World...

I. Writing check.

Write a postcard to a friend about Angkor Wat.

```
POSTCARD                                    [stamp: 1500R ROYAUME DU CAMBODGE]

                                    _____

                                    _____

                                    _____

                                    _____
```

J. Pronunciation check.

Look at the flag,
What do you see?
Angkor Wat!
The beautiful temple
The Cambodian people
of Angkor Wat
of Cambodia,

the Cambodian flag.
What do we see?
Angkor Wat?
of Angkor Wat!
are very, very proud
on their flag,
of Kampuchea.

K. Talk about in small groups.

Would you like to visit Cambodia? Why?
What do you know about Cambodia's history?
Where is it? Tell us about it.

L. What's next for Igor?

(rrrrring)

Susan: Bob's Scuba Dive Center. May I help you?

Igor: Hello, is Bob there?

Susan: He's out on the Barrier Reef.

Igor: Who am I speaking to?

Susan: Susan.

Igor: Well, uh, Susan, can you give Bob a message?

Susan: Sure.

Igor: Tell him Igor will arrive Monday from Cambodia.

Susan: He knows you're coming?

Igor: Not exactly.

Susan: I see. Well, I'll tell Bob.

Igor: Thanks. See you Monday.

M. Check the Internet: <en.wikipedia.org/wiki/AngkorWat>

17

underwater at the
Great Barrier Reef

PHOTOGRAPHER: DAN HARE | AGENCY: DREAMSTIME.COM

WHAT? a coral reef   **WHERE:** Australian coast

HOW MANY YEARS? millions   **HOW LONG?** 1,250 miles

WHO? Australians and tourists   **WHY?** to swim and dive

A. Where's Igor?

(rrrrring)

Igor: Hello.

You: Igor! Where have you been ? I've tried to call you.

Igor: I've been underwater.

You: Underwater? Are you in a submarine?

Igor: No. I'm diving.

You: Where, for heaven's sake?

Igor: On the Great Barrier Reef in Australia!

You: Really! What a great place to be!

Igor: You bet, mate!

You: How long ...

Igor: Sorry. I'm going under again. OK, Susan, let's go! (splash)

You: Igor! Igor! Argh ...

B. Do you know these words?

a barrier _____

a reef _____

a shell _____

to remain _____

to form _____

an island _____

a surface _____

fantastic _____

to swim _____

colorful _____

C. Read.

The Great Barrier Reef is along the northeast coast of Australia. It was built up over millions of years by tiny sea animals. These animals make limestone shells (coral). When they die, the shell remains. Millions of them have lived, died, and formed an island or a reef. The reef is at or just below the surface. The Great Barrier Reef is the largest coral reef in the world. It is 1,250 miles long. It is a fantastic place. Australians and tourists like to swim and dive here. They see colorful fish and unusual forms. The coral has many beautiful colors, and it is used for jewelry. (108)

D. Match the question with an answer.

1. ___ What country?   A. biggest in the world
2. ___ What kind of reef?   B. colorful
3. ___ How many tiny animals?   C. millions of years
4. ___ How long is the reef?   D. Australia
5. ___ How old is the reef?   E. Australians, tourists
6. ___ What kind of fish?   F. coral (or barrier)
7. ___ How big is the reef?   G. millions
8. ___ Who likes to swim?   H. 1,250 miles

E. Write the answer.

1. What kind of reef is it? _____

2. Where is it? _____

3. What made it? _____

4. How long is the reef? _____

5. Why do people go there? _____

F. Grammar check. Use: *doesn't* or *don't*.

1. John _____ like to dive.

2. Tom and I _____ like to dive.

3. He _____ travel every year.

4. They _____ like to travel to unusual places.

5. We _____ go to unusual places.

6. Bob _____ want to swim, but I do.

7. Tom _____ have to travel.

G. Word check. Use these words: *barrier, reef, coast, shell, coral, remains, formed, islands, surface, fantastic, Divers, colorful*

1. There are many _____ in the sea.

2. The animals' limestone _____ is called _____.

3. The _____ is a 1,250-mile-long _____.

4. These tiny animals have _____ a huge reef.

5. People swim on the _____ of the sea.

6. _____ like to swim underwater.

7. The Great Barrier Reef is along the Australian _____.

8. When the animal dies, the shell _____.

9. The reef is a beautiful and _____ place. The colors are _____.

H. Listen and write.

1. _____

2. _____

3. _____

4. _____

5. _____

I. Writing check.

Write a postcard to a friend about the Great Barrier Reef.

J. Pronunciation check.

Let's go diving,
under the sea,
Let's go see
We'll go see
What'll we see there?
Colorful life,
under the sea,
Fantastic life
under the sea,

diving, diving
the beautiful sea!
the coral reef.
the long coral reef!
What will be there?
fantastic life,
right under the sea.
there to see
for you and me.

K. Talk about it in small groups.

Would you like to go to the Great Barrier Reef?
Do you like to swim? Where do you swim?
Would you like to go underwater diving?
What's the best beach that you know of? Where is it?

L. What's up with Igor?

(rrrrring)

Bob:	Hello?
Igor:	Hi, Bob. How's it going?
Bob:	Good. What's up?
Igor:	I just wanted to say thanks again for putting me up. I had a fantastic time.
Bob:	My pleasure, Igor. Next time I'm in Boston, I'll look you up.
Igor:	You're always welcome.
Bob:	I hope you and Susan have a great time in Hawaii.
Igor:	We will, Bob.
Bob:	Is she going to teach you surfing, too?
Igor:	Well, I don't know about that.
Bob:	Anyway, mate, have fun. I've a call on the other line.

M. Check the Internet: <www.gbrmpa.gov.au>

18

Aloha from Hawaii!

WHAT? volcanoes   HOW MANY? two

WHERE? national park   WHO? visitors

WHY? to look, see, camp, hike   WHEN? 1916

A. Where's Igor?

(rrrrring)

Igor: Hello!

You: Hello, Igor. Bob called. He said you are in Hawaii.

Igor: I'm in beautiful Hawaii.

You: What are you doing there?

Igor: I'm visiting Volcanoes National Park.

You: Really? Volcanoes?

Igor: Yes, red-hot, active volcanoes!

You: But I thought you were surfing with Susan.

Igor: I was.

You: What happened?

Igor: She met an old surfer friend, and ... well, anyway, I didn't like surfing.

You: I see. Well, don't get too close to those craters.

Igor: Hmm. The ... the ... g-g-gr-ground is sh-sha-sh-a-king. I ... I'd b-b-bet ... ter ... r-r-r-run!!!!

B. Do you know these words?

a volcano _____

active _____

lava _____

to bubble _____

to flow _____

to pray _____

a gift _____

public _____

C. Read.

Hawaii Volcanoes National Park is an unusual place. It was formed by five volcanoes. Two are still active. One is Mauna Loa and the other is Kilauea. Kilauea is more active. On Kilauea you can actually see the red-hot lava bubbling and flowing slowly in the crater. Many Hawaiians believe that Pele lives here. She is the Goddess of the volcano. They pray to her, and they leave gifts to her to keep her quiet. A lot of visitors come here to look at the volcano. The national park is very large and you can hike and camp in it. In 1916, it became a public park for all to enjoy. (112)

D. Answer: *Yes, I agree.* or *No, I disagree.*

1. Hawaii Volcanoes is a national park. _____

2. Five volcanoes are active. _____

3. Pele is a volcano. _____

4. Kilauea has red-hot lava. _____

5. Mauna Loa is an active volcano. _____

6. People cannot see the hot lava. _____

7. You cannot camp in the park. _____

8. The Park was established 1816. _____

E. Write the answer.

1. What is Hawaii Volcanoes National Park? _____

2. Where is it? _____

3. Who goes there? _____

4. Why do they go? _____

5. When did it become a park? _____

F. Grammar check. Use: *There is / Is there* or *There are / Are there*

Example: *There are* five volcanoes.

1. _____ two active volcanoes.

2. _____ red-hot lava in the crater.

3. _____ many campers?

4. _____ many visitors.

5. _____ a public park on Hawaii ?

6. _____ many islands?

7. _____ many hikers in the park.

G. Word check. Fill in the blanks with the following words: *volcanoes, active, lava, bubbles, flows, pray, gifts, hike, camp, public*

1. The _____ is red and hot.

2. There are two _____ volcanoes.

3. The lava _____ and _____.

4. People can _____ and _____ in the park.

5. Hawaiians leave _____ for Pele and _____ to her.

6. A national park is a _____ place.

7. There are _____ on the island of Hawaii.

H. Listen and write.

1. _____

2. _____

3. _____

4. _____

5. _____

I. Writing check.

Write a postcard to a friend about Hawaii.

postcard

25 USA

CAPE HATTERAS, NORTH CAROLINA

_____

_____

_____

_____

Pele is waiting.

J. Pronunciation check.

Red-hot lava!
Bubbling in the crater,
down the mountainside,
Red and black
flowing and bubbling

Red-hot, and black!
flowing from the crater,
down the mountainside.
and dangerous lava,
down the mountainside!

K. Talk about it in small groups.

What other volcanoes do you know about?

Are they active?

Would you like to go to Hawaii? Why?

L. Where's Igor going?

Igor: Aloha.

Susan: Hey, Igor, I'm back in Australia.

Igor: That's nice.

Susan: How were the volcanoes?

Igor: They were fantastic! How was the surfing?

Susan: The surf was good. You should have tried it.

Igor: Maybe next time.

Susan: Are you coming back to Australia?

Igor: I'm not. I'm going to get away from it all.

Susan: Where are you going?

Igor: I'm not telling anyone.

Susan: Oh. Well, good luck.

Igor: Thanks. Take care.

M. Check the Internet: <www.gohawaii.com>

Easter Island
Chile

19

WHAT? statues

WHERE? an island
South Pacific Ocean
Chilean coast

HOW FAR? 2,237 miles

WHO? Polynesians

WHEN? 400 – 1600 C.E.

HOW MANY? about 887

HOW TALL? some are 40 feet

HOW MANY PEOPLE NOW? about 3,800

PHOTOGRAPHER: © ASTRA 490 | AGENCY: DREAMSTIME.COM

A. Where's Igor?

(rrrrring)

Igor: Hello!

You: Hello! At last I've found you! Where are you?

Igor: I'm on Easter Island.

You: Really? Eastern Island? Where's that?

Igor: It's thousands of miles from Chile. And it's <u>Easter</u> Island.

You: What are you doing there?

Igor: I'm looking at some really strange, big heads.

You: Really? Heads? Of people?

Igor: Statues with big heads and no eyes. Hundreds of them.

You: Wow! I'd like to see them.

Igor: Google Easter Island.

You: OK, I'll do that. Take care.

Igor: Bye bye.

B. Do you know these words?

isolated _____

to belong to _____

strange _____

approximately _____

others _____

a mystery _____

about _____

the rest _____

to depend on _____

C. Read.

Easter Island is a small, isolated island in the South Pacific. It belongs to Chile, but it is 2,237 miles from the Chilean coast. There are huge stone statues on Easter Island. They are strange. They have big heads and no eyes. Some are 40 feet tall. There are approximately 887 statues on the island. Nobody knows why or when they were built. Some people think Polynesians made them about 400 C.E. Others think they were made between 1100 and 1600 C.E. They are a mystery. Today about 3,500 people live on Easter Island. About 60 percent of them are Polynesians. The rest are Chileans. Their economy depends on tourism. (109)

D. Answer: *Yes, of course!* or *No, not really!*

1. Does Easter Island have stone statues? _____

2. Are the statues big? _____

3. Do the statues look like animals? _____

4. Is Easter Island in the Atlantic Ocean? _____

5. Does Easter Island belong to Hawaii? _____

6. Is Easter Island in the Pacific Ocean? _____

7. Are the statues very small? _____

8. Are the statues a mystery? _____

E. Write the answer.

What do the statues look like?
Where are they?
Who made the statues?
When were they made?
Why were they made?

F. Grammar check. Use *some* or *any*

1. They don't have _____ eyes.

2. I didn't see _____ .

3. _____ of them are tall.

4. _____ statues are not so tall.

5. _____ people live on the island.

6. Do they have _____ tourism?

7. They have _____ tourists in the winter.

8. Do they have _____ in the summer?

G. Word check. Fill in the blanks: *isolated, belongs to, strange, Approximately, Others, mystery, about, The rest, depends on*

1. There are huge, _____ statues on Easter Island.

2. Why were they made? It's a _____ .

3. Some think they are very old. _____ don't think so.

4. Forty percent are Chilean. _____ are Polynesians.

5. Easter Island is very _____ ; it's _____ 2,300 miles from Chile.

6. _____ 3,500 people live there.

7. Easter Island _____ Chile.

8. The island _____ tourism.

H. Listen and write.

1. _____

2. _____

3. _____

4. _____

5. _____

I. Writing check.

Write a postcard to a friend about Easter Island.

postcard

PHOTOGRAPHER: © UWE BLOSFELD

AGENCY: DREAMSTIME.COM

SESQUICENTENARIO DE LA TOMA DE VALDIVIA POR LORD COCHRANE · 1820 - 1970

40 CTS   CORREOS DE CHILE

J. Pronunciation check.

Look at these	big stone statues!
Look at these	big, big heads!
Big stone statues	with no eyes.
Big, big heads,	none with eyes.
Can't believe it!	What a place!
Easter Island!	Easter Island!
Far, far away!	Far, far away!

K. Talk about it in small groups.

Why do you think these statues were made?

Why are they so big?

Would you like to go to Easter Island? Why or why not?

What are some other islands you know about?

L. It's Igor, leaving Easter Island!

(rrrrring)

You: Hello?

Igor: Hi. I just want you to know that I'm going to a place where my cell phone probably won't work.

You: Where in the world is that?

Igor: I'm leaving the island tomorrow and flying to Argentina.

You: But your phone should work in Argentina.

Igor: I know, but I want to join an expedition to the South Pole.

You: What! You are crazy, aren't you?

Igor: I'm trying to find peace and quiet.

You: Well, you have seen a lot. Maybe it's time to come home.

Igor: Not yet. There's more to see, and Antarctica is next.

You: You're nuts!

Igor: Maybe. Talk to you when I get back.

M. Check the Internet: <www.netaxs.com-trance/rapanui.html>

20

WHAT?	Antarctica a continent	**WHERE?**	the South Pole
WHO?	explorers scientists tourists	**WHY?**	to explore to study to see
WHEN?	1911		

A. It's Igor!

(rrrrring)

Igor: Hello!

You: Hello, Igor? How was Antarctica?

Igor: I didn't go.

You: What happened?

Igor: It's mid-June, right?

You: Right.

Igor: So there's no sunlight. It's completely dark.

You: Of course! So what will you do?

Igor: I'm going to hang out for a few days here in Buenos Aires.

You: That's nice. What will you do there?

Igor: I'm going to learn how to tango.

You: But it takes two to tango.

Igor: I know. Here comes my instructor. Bye.

B. Do you know these words?

continent _____

lonely _____

to cover _____

an ice sheet _____

to surround _____

a penguin _____

a seal _____

an explorer _____

to freeze _____

C. Read.

Antarctica is at the South Pole. It's the coldest; it's the windiest; it's the darkest; it's the driest place on earth. It's the highest continent, and it is a very lonely place. It is covered by an ice sheet and surrounded by icy waters. However, penguins and seals live there. Humans never lived there. However, scientists come to study it, and tourists come to see it. Why do tourists want to go there? Because it is very different, and it is beautiful in a special way. Roald Amundsen was the first man to go to the South Pole in 1911. He was an explorer. Later other explorers came. Some froze to death! (114)

D. Answer: *Yes, that's right!* **or** *No, that's not right at all!*

1. Antarctica is a city. _____

2. It is at the North Pole. _____

3. It has strong winds. _____

4. Many people live there. _____

5. Scientists go to Antarctica. _____

6. Antarctica has penguins. _____

7. You can swim there. _____

8. Explorers came to Antarctica in 1611. _____

E. Write the answer.

1. What is Antarctica? _____

2. Where is Antarctica? _____

3. Who lives there? _____

4. Why do scientists go there ? _____

5. When did Amundsen go there? _____

Antarctica

F. Grammar check. Write the *–est* form of these words.

Example: *It's a big place.* > <u>*In fact, it's the biggest place.*</u>

1. It's a dry place. _____

2. Is it a windy place? _____

3. I think it's a cold place. _____

4. It's a dark place. _____

5. Is it high? _____

6. Is it a lonely place? _____

7. Is it an icy place? _____

G. Word check. Use: *continent, lonely, covered, sheet, surrounds, penguin, Seals, froze, explorer*

1. A person who likes to go to new places is an _____.

2. Antarctica is a _____.

3. It was so cold he _____ to death!

4. This bird lives in Antarctica. It is the _____.

5. Antarctica is _____ with an ice _____.

6. Icy water _____ Antarctica.

7. Nobody lives there; it's a very _____ place.

8. _____ also live there. They eat penguins.

H. Listen and write.

1. _____

2. _____

3. _____

4. _____

5. _____

Where in the World...

I. Writing check.

Write a postcard to a friend from Argentina.

greetings from
the bottom of the world!

EL SELLO POSTAL DIBUJO
CORREOS
10 / 10 CENTAVOS
EXPOSICION FILATELICA INTERNACIONAL
REPUBLICA ARGENTINA

PHOTOGRAPHER: © STEVE ESTVANIK | AGENCY: DREAMSTIME.COM

J. Pronunciation check.

Brrr! Brrr! It's cold, it's cold!
Brrr! Brr! I'm shivering.
Teeth are chattering,
I'm really, really cold!
windiest, driest
Cold and wind
Cold and windy,
the loneliest place.
in Antarctica!
Brrr! Brrr!

Really, really cold!
Really, really shivering!
chattering, chattering!
It's the coldest, highest,
place on earth.
and icy weather.
Antarctica is
Way, way down
In Antarctica!
it's really, really cold!

K. Talk about it in small groups.

Would you like to visit Antarctica? Why or why not?
What would you need to take?
What would you see?

L. Where will Igor go?

(rrrrring)

You: Hello.

Igor: It's me again. I'm off to Brazil.

You: So can you tango now?

Igor: My instructor was great.

You: But did you learn to tango?

Igor: Well, I did all right.

You: I bet!

Igor: So I'll call you from Brazil. We leave in half an hour.

You: We?

Igor: Here she comes. Talk to you later.

M. Check the Internet: < en.wikipedia.org/wiki/Antarctica >

21

PHOTOGRAPHER: © NICOLA VEERNIZZI | AGENCY: DREAMSTIME.COM

Amazon Magic

WHAT? Amazon rainforest	**WHERE?** Brazil, Amazon
HOW BIG? huge	**HOW HOT?** very
WHAT KIND? strange, colorful	**HOW WET?** very
WHO? ranchers, loggers	**WHY?** for cattle, wood

A. Where's Igor?

(rrrrring)

Igor: Hello?

You: Hello, Igor? Are you in Brazil?

Igor: I'm in the Amazon Rainforest.

You: Really? You aren't in Rio?

Igor: That's right!

You: What are you doing there?

Igor: I'm on a river boat.

You: Are you on the Amazon River?

Igor: We are. Maria is taking pictures of the amazing birds and monkeys.

You: Well, enjoy!

Igor: We will!

B. Do you know these words?

the earth _____

to grow _____

fast _____

dense _____

to shrink _____

to clear _____

a planet _____

lungs _____

to breathe _____

health _____

C. Read.

The Amazon Rainforest is huge. It is the biggest one on earth. It is hot. It rains a lot. It's very green. Everything grows fast here. The Rainforest is very dense. It's hard to walk because the trees and plants are very close together. You can see strange animals and colorful birds. It's like no other place on earth.

Today the Amazon Rainforest is shrinking because ranchers are clearing the land for cattle, and loggers are cutting the trees for wood. So the Amazon Rainforest is getting smaller and smaller. This is not good for the people on Planet Earth. The Rainforest is the lungs of the planet. The forest breathes in carbon dioxide and breathes out oxygen. The Rainforest is necessary for our health! (125)

D. Answer: *Yes, that's certainly true.* **or** *No, that's definitely wrong.*

1. The Amazon is in Brazil. _____

2. The Rainforest is very large. _____

3. Few birds and animals live there. _____

4. The Rainforest has little rain. _____

5. It is cold in the Rainforest. _____

6. The Rainforest is getting larger. _____

7. People are cutting the trees. _____

E. Write the answer.

1. What is the Amazon? _____

2. Where is the Rainforest? _____

3. Who is cutting down the trees? Why? _____

4. How big is the rainforest? _____

5. Why is it important? _____

F. Grammar check. Use the words to write a question.

Example: *you .. walk .. forest .. now.* <u>*Are you walking in the forest now?*</u>

1. she .. take .. photos _____ ?

2. they .. cut .. trees .. now _____ ?

3. forest .. get .. smaller _____ ?

4. people .. clear .. land _____ ?

5. we .. look at .. animals _____ ?

6. I .. leave .. with you _____ ?

7. forest .. grow .. fast _____ ?

G. Word check. Fill in the blanks with these words: *Earth, grow, fast, dense, shrinking, ranchers, clearing, cattle, Loggers, wood, planets, lungs, breathe, healthy*

1. The Rainforest is very _____.

2. Ranchers are _____ the land for _____.

3. _____ is one of the _____.

4. The forest is _____ very rapidly.

5. Plants grow very _____ here.

6. We _____ with our _____.

7. Do we need to _____ more food?

8. A _____ Earth needs the Rainforest.

9. _____ cut trees for _____.

H. Listen and write.

1. _____

2. _____

3. _____

4. _____

5. _____

I. Writing check.

Write a postcard to a friend about the Amazon Rainforest.

J. Pronunciation check.

Do you want to see
strange-looking monkeys?   Yes, we do. Yes, we do.
Unusual birds?   Yes, we do. Yes, we do.
Do you want to see
a deep, dense forest?   Yes, of course. Yes, of course.
Go to the Rainforest.   Where is that?
The Amazon, the Amazon!   In Brazil?
In Brazil. The place for you!   We'll go. We'll go. How about you?
I'll come too! I'll come too!   Let's all go! Let's do! Let's do!

K. Talk about it in small groups.

Would you like to visit the Amazon Rainforest?

Are rainforests important? Why or why not?

What kind of animals are in the Rainforest?

What kind of forests does your country or state have?

Do you like to walk in the forest?

L. It's Igor!

(rrrrring)

Igor: Hola, Pablo! It's me, Igor!

Pablo: No way! I thought you were in China.

Igor: I was a few weeks ago. Guess where I am now.

Pablo: Don't tell me you're here in Peru.

Igor: Well, not quite. I'm stuck in the Amazon with a friend.

Pablo: What happened?

Igor: Our boat hit a rock, and we missed our flight from Manaus.

Pablo: So where were you going?

Igor: Guess!

Pablo: Huh! You're coming here to Peru, aren't you?

Igor: You guessed it.

Pablo: OK. Call me when you get here.

Igor: Will do.

M. Check the Internet: <www.amazon-rainforest.org>

Where in the World...

Machu Picchu
Peru

22

Among the clouds

WHAT? an ancient city

WHERE? Peru

WHO? the Inca

WHEN? 15th century

WHY? for ceremonies

PHOTOGRAPHER: © GALYNA ANDRUSHKO | AGENCY: DREAMSTIME.COM

A. Where's Igor?

(rrrrring)

Igor: Hello!

You: Hello! Where are you?

Igor: I'm in Peru.

You: What are you doing there?

Igor: I'm visiting the ancient city of Machu Picchu with Pablo and Maria.

You: Interesting?

Igor: Yes, very, very interesting!

You: Well, take some pictures.

Igor: Guess what! I lost my camera.

You: Oh, Igor. Too bad! Anyway, have a good time.

Igor: Adiós.

B. Do you know these words?

lost _____

a culture _____

perhaps _____

a place _____

close _____

the sky _____

popular _____

a ceremony _____

to attract _____

C. Read.

In the high, high Andes Mountains of Peru, there is an ancient city. It is Machu Picchu. Nobody lives there today, but many people visit it. The Inca Indians built it a long time ago, maybe in the fifteenth century. For a long time nobody knew that it was there. It was a lost city. But why did they build it so high in the mountains? Perhaps ancient cultures thought that mountains were special places. Mountains are tall and close to the sky. Maybe they thought gods and goddesses lived in the sky. Some people think the Inca built it as a special place for ceremonies. However, nobody really knows for sure. Today it attracts tourists from all around the world. (121)

D. Answer: *This sentence is OK.* or *This sentence is not OK.*

1. Machu Picchu is a new city. _____

2. Machu Picchu is a very old city. _____

3. Machu Picchu is a country. _____

4. Machu Picchu is by the ocean. _____

5. It is in Brazil. _____

6. The Spanish built it. _____

7. The Inca built Machu Picchu. _____

E. Write the answer.

1. What is Machu Picchu? _____

2. Where is Machu Picchu? _____

3. Who were the Inca? _____

4. When did the Inca build it? _____

5. Why did they build it? _____

F. Grammar check. Make the following sentences negative.

Example: *The Inca were in Brazil.* *The Inca weren't in Brazil.*

1. The Incas were Spanish. _____

2. Machu Picchu was a country. _____

3. Machu Picchu was a Spanish city. _____

4. The Incas were Brazilians. _____

5. Machu Picchu was a park. _____

6. The builders were the Maya. _____

G. Word check. Fill in the blanks with these words: *lost, culture, Perhaps, place, close, sky, popular, ceremonies, attracts*

1. It is a fascinating and special _____.

2. For many years it was _____.

3. The Incan _____ is very old.

4. Why did they build it? _____ it was for _____.

5. They thought gods lived in the _____. The Inca wanted to be _____ to the gods.

6. It is a _____ tourist place today.

7. It _____ many tourists.

H. Listen and write.

1. _____

2. _____

3. _____

4. _____

5. _____

Where in the World...

I. Writing check.

Write a postcard to a friend about Machu Picchu.

missing you in
Machu Picchu

PERU
CORREOS
100

1981

AÑO INTERNACIONAL DE LOS IMPEDIDOS

J. Pronunciation check.

You can walk to the top.

Or take a bus.

Almost to the top.

Doesn't matter to me.

Just want to see,

what the Inca built,

a long time ago.

It's really quite a hike!

All the way to the top?

So which will it be?

And I don't care!

just you and me,

what was built by the Inca

Centuries ago!

K. Talk about it in small groups.

Would you like to visit Machu Picchu? Why or why not?
What native people do you know about? Where are they?
Do you know anything about the Mayas or the Aztecs?

J. It's Igor!

(rrrring)

Pablo: Diga.

Igor: Hola, Pablo!

Pablo: Hi, Igor, what's up?

Igor: Well, first, thanks for showing us Machu Picchu.

Pablo: Don't mention it. How's Maria?

Igor: She's on her way back to Argentina.

Pablo: Oh, really?

Igor: And I was on my way to Ecuador, but I have a problem.

Pablo: Oh?

Igor: Um, I lost my wallet.

Pablo: Oh no!

Igor: So, can I ...

Pablo: Listen, Igor, I can't talk right now. Call me at home tonight.

Igor: But ...

(click)

M. Check the Internet: <en.wikipedia.org/wiki/Machu_Picchu>

HOLA FROM THE GALAPAGOS ISLANDS

WHAT? islands

WHERE? Pacific Ocean

WHAT? wildlife

WHAT KIND? strange, unique

WHO? Charles Darwin

WHY? to study the wildlife

WHO? tourists

WHY? to see the wildlife

A. Where's Igor?

(rrrrring)

Igor: Hello.

You: Hello. Where are you?

Igor: I'm in the Galapagos Islands.

You: Really, what are you doing?

Igor: I'm looking at strange birds and animals.

You: Interesting?

Igor: Yes, very interesting, but I'm going to start ... running.

You: What's happening!

Igor: A ... very ... large ... iguana ... is ... (click)

B. Do you know these words?

unique _____

powerful _____

to fly _____

to weigh _____

a lizard _____

to develop _____

evolution _____

near _____

to bother _____

a threat _____

C. Read.

The Galapagos Islands are in the Pacific Ocean. They are on the equator, 600 miles from the coast of Ecuador. They were formed by an underwater volcano. Strange and unique birds and animals live there. There is a bird, the cormorant. It is big and powerful. It dives for fish but it cannot fly. There are huge tortoises. They weigh over 500 pounds! And there are thousands of lizards called iguanas. Charles Darwin came here many years ago to study the Islands' wildlife. His studies helped him develop his ideas about evolution.

Today, many tourists visit the islands all year. They walk around and near the animals. They are careful not to bother the animals. However, tourism can be a threat to the unique wildlife of the islands. (128)

D. Match the two parts of the sentence.

1. _____ The Galapagos Islands
2. _____ They are 600 miles
3. _____ They were formed
4. _____ The strange cormorant
5. _____ It dives
6. _____ The tortoises
7. _____ Many tourists
8. _____ Tourism

A. cannot fly.
B. visit the islands.
C. is a threat.
D. from the coast.
E. are huge.
F. for fish.
G. by a volcano.
H. are in the Pacific.

E. Write the answer.

1. What are the Galapagos? _____

2. Where are they? _____

3. Who comes here? _____

4. Why do they come? _____

5. How often do they come? _____

F. Grammar check. Use: *They* or *There*.

1. _____ are 13 main islands.

2. _____ are 600 miles from the coast.

3. _____ are many strange animals there.

4. _____ are hundreds of tortoises on the islands.

5. _____ are huge.

6. _____ are thousands of lizards.

7. _____ are called iguanas.

G. Word check. Fill in the blanks. Use these words: *unique, powerful, fly, weigh, lizard, developed, evolution, bother, threatens*

1. The cormorant can swim and dive, but it cannot _____.

2. The tortoises _____ a lot.

3. The iguana is a strange looking _____, and it is a very

_____ swimmer.

4. Please don't _____ the animals.

5. Too much tourism _____ the wildlife.

6. They _____ a program to protect the wildlife.

7. Darwin developed the theory of _____.

8. Most of the wildlife on the islands is _____.

H. Listen and write.

1. _____

2. _____

3. _____

4. _____

5. _____

Where in the World...

I. Writing check.

Write a postcard to a friend about the Galapagos Islands.

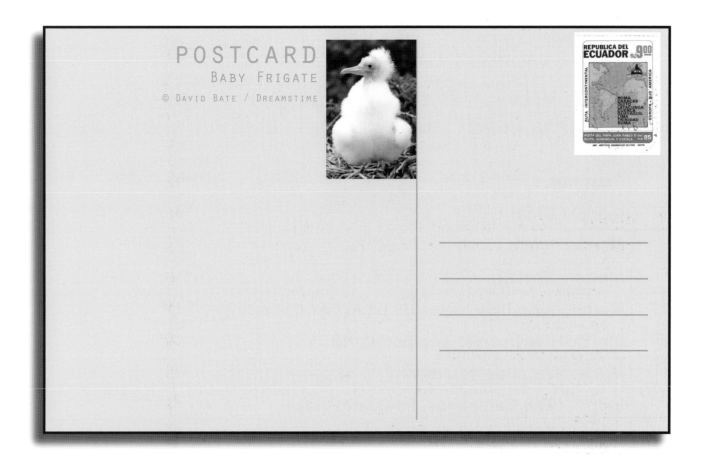

POSTCARD

BABY FRIGATE

© DAVID BATE / DREAMSTIME

REPUBLICA DEL
ECUADOR S/.9.00

J. Pronunciation practice.

Big birds there.

And lizards, too.

And lizards, too!

They're very, very big

They're very, very old!

The Galapagos Islands.

And waiting for you!

The Galapagos.

Strange birds there.

And lizards, too?

And how about tortoises?

and very, very old.

In the Galapagos?

They're waiting there.

They're waiting for us!

The Galapagos.

K. Group conversations.

Would you like to visit Galapagos? Why?
What kind of animals do you like?
Where do they live?
Is a zoo a good place for animals?

L. It's Igor, isn't it?

(rrrrring)

Igor: Diga!

Maria: Igor?

Igor: Maria?

Maria: Igor, how have you been? And where?

Igor: I've been to another world.

Maria: What do you mean?

Igor: The Galapagos. Fantastic place!

Maria: So I've heard. You're so lucky.

Igor: Well, uh, sort of.

Maria: Oh?

Igor: Yeah. I ate something bad.

Maria: Oh. Diarrhea?

Igor: Yeah. Uh, oh, Maria. I've got to go!

M. Check the Internet: < www.worldwildlife.org/galapagos>

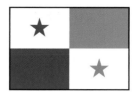

24

WHAT? a canal

WHERE? Panama

HOW LONG? over 50 miles

WHO? French, Americans

WHEN? 1880-1914

WHY? to connect two oceans

A. Where's Igor?

(rrrrring)

Igor: Hello!

You: Hello, Igor? Where are you?

Igor: I'm in Panama.

You: Are you traveling in Central America now?

Igor: Actually, I'm on a boat. I'm going through the Panama Canal.

You: Really? Well, where are you going?

Igor: I'm taking a cruise ship to Mexico.

You: Mexico?

Igor: Si, si! Cancún, here I come! Adiós, amigo.

You: Adiós!

B. Do you know these words?

to connect _____

a dream _____

to fail _____

to complete _____

expensive _____

malaria _____

an accident _____

construction _____

to use _____

to save _____

C. Read.

The Panama Canal connects the Pacific Ocean with the Atlantic Ocean. It is just over 50 miles long. For many years, building a canal across Panama was only a dream. Many countries wanted to find a way from one ocean to the other. First, the French tried in 1880, but they failed. Finally, the United States completed it in 1914. But it was very expensive. Thousands of workers died. They died from malaria and accidents. About 30,000 people died during the construction.

Today ships use the canal for business and travel. Ships traveling from New York to San Francisco save 7,872 miles, and it takes only 8 to 10 hours to go through the canal. On January 1, 2000, the United States finally gave the canal back to Panama. (129)

D. Answer. Match the question with an answer.

1. _____ What does the Canal connect?   A. thousands
2. _____ How long is the canal?   B. 1880
3. _____ What country failed to build it?   C. from malaria and accidents
4. _____ When did they begin?   D. Panama
5. _____ When was it completed?   E. two oceans
6. _____ How many workers died?   F. about 50 miles
7. _____ Why did they die?   G. France
8. _____ Who does the canal belong to?   H. 1914

E. Write the answers.

1. Where is the Panama Canal?_____

2. Who built it? _____

3. Why was it built?_____

4. When was it built?_____

5. When was it finished? _____

F. Grammar check. Use _yes_ or _no_ answers.

1. Did the U.S. complete the Panama Canal? _Yes, it did._

2. Did Panama build the Canal? _____

3. In 1850 did ships travel around South America? _____

4. Did many workers die? _____

5. Did they die from disease? _____

6. Did the canal take fifty years to build? _____

7. Did the U.S. give the canal to Panama in 1950? _____

G. Word check. Fill in the blanks. Use: _connects, dream, failed, complete, expensive, accidents, Malaria, construction, use, save_

1. The Panama Canal _____ two oceans.

2. It was an _____ and dangerous _____.

3. Many workers died from _____ and malaria.

4. Many ships _____ the canal.

5. Today, the Canal is real; it is not a _____.

6. The French _____ to _____ the canal.

7. Ships using the canal _____ thousands of miles.

8. _____ is a disease.

H. Listen and write.

1. _____

2. _____

3. _____

4. _____

5. _____

Where in the World...

I. Writing check.

Write a postcard to a friend about the Panama Canal.

Greetings from
the Panama Canal

panamá 6¢

Ara severa "loro"

_____

_____

_____

_____

J. Pronunciation check.

Imagine! Imagine
digging a canal,
with food so bad
and hungry, hungry,
making workers sick,
But still they worked
Fifty miles
till the job was done.

digging a canal,
in weather so hot
and work so hard
big mosquitoes
sick with malaria.
and never stopped.
from Atlantic to Pacific
Till the job was done!

K. Talk about it in small groups.

Why are canals important?

Do you know about other canals? Where?

Would you like to visit the Panama Canal? Why or why not?

L. It's Igor!

Lupita: Bueno.

Igor: Hola, Lupita!

Lupita: No! It can't be! It's you, isn't it, Igor?

Igor: It's me, all right.

Lupita: Where are you? And, um, why are you calling?

Igor: Well, to invite you to join me in Cancún.

Lupita: Cancún? You? But that's hours from Mexico City.

Igor: I can wait. In fact, I'm going to Chichen Itza today.

Lupita: Why don't you come here?

Igor: Great idea. Thanks for inviting me. Can you make a reservation for me at a hotel for tomorrow?

Lupita: Uh, OK, but ...

Igor: Here comes the tour bus. See you tomorrow.

M. Check the Internet: <www.canalmuseum.com>

25

PHOTOGRAPHER: © CAROLINA K. SMITH, M.D. | AGENCY: DREAM-

WHAT? an ancient city

WHERE? Mexico

WHO? the Maya

WHEN? 300-800 C.E.

A. Where's Igor?

(rrrrring)

Igor: Bueno.

You: Where are you now, Igor?

Igor: On top of a pyramid.

You: Did you go back to Egypt?

Igor: No, I'm in Mexico.

You: What are you doing there?

Igor: I climbed up a big pyramid — El Castillo!

You: Where's that?

Igor: At Chichen Itza. I'm starting to climb down. I've got to be careful. Talk to you later.

B. Do you know these words?

a peninsula _____

to establish _____

skillful _____

complex _____

a system _____

accurate _____

a calendar _____

a descendant _____

a ceremony _____

C. Read.

Chichen Itza is a very old Mayan city in Mexico. It is on the Yucatán peninsula. It was established in 514 C.E. by the Maya. The Maya were Native American Indians. They lived in Central America and in Mexico between 300 and 800 C.E. They were skillful architects. They designed and built many interesting buildings. They also developed a complex writing system and accurate calendars. Their descendants still live there today.

In the center of Chichen Itza is El Castillo. It is a pyramid. It was built for a Mayan king. It is 75 feet tall. It was used for many different ceremonies. You can climb to the top of the pyramid. Many people come to see and walk around Chichen Itza. They wonder how the Maya made these beautiful buildings so many years ago. (135)

D. Answer: *Yes, that's correct.* **or** *No, that's incorrect.*

1. El Castillo is a city. _____

2. El Castillo is a pyramid. _____

3. Chichen Itza was built by the Maya. _____

4. It was built 1,000 years ago. _____

5. Chichen Itza is in Mexico. _____

6. The Maya had a writing system. _____

E. Write the answer.

1. What is Chichen Itza?_____

2. Where is El Castillo?_____

3. Who were the Maya? _____

4. Why did they build El Castillo? _____

5. When did the Maya live there? _____

Chichen Itza

F. Grammar check. Make questions. Use: *Was* or *Were*.

1. _____ the Maya good architects?

2. _____ it built a long time ago?

3. _____ El Castillo a Spanish church?

4. _____ the Maya Native Americans?

5. _____ the writing system complex?

6. _____ Chichen Itza a city?

7. _____ the Maya also in Central America?

8. _____ Chichen Itza established in 1500 C.E?

G. Word check. Fill the blanks. Use: *Peninsula, established, skillful, complex, system, accurate, calendar, Descendants, ceremonies*

1. The Maya had a _____ writing _____.

2. The Yucatán _____ has a sea on three sides.

3. Chichen Itza was _____ in the sixth century C.E.

4. The Maya architects were very _____.

5. _____ of the Maya still live in Mexico.

6. El Castillo was probably used for _____.

7. Their _____ was very _____.

H. Listen and write.

1. _____

2. _____

3. _____

4. _____

5. _____

I. Writing check.

Write a postcard to a friend about Chichen Itza.

IT'S A NOTE
FROM CHICHEN ITZA

$10

J. Pronunciation check.

Chichen Itza!
A city, a city!
built by the Maya?
so long ago.
so long ago?
In Mexico!
in Mexico.

Chichen Itza!
An ancient city,
Built by the Maya
How did they do it
So long ago!
A long time ago
We don't know.

K. Talk about it.

Do you know another place like Chichen Itza?
Where is it?
Is it unusual? In what way?
Would you like to go to Mexico?
What would you like to see?

L. It's Igor.

(rrrrring)

Lupita: Mande.

Igor: Hi, Lupita.

Lupita: So, Igor, are you at your hotel?

Igor: I am, but my luggage isn't.

Lupita: What happened?

Igor: I don't know. Can you help me?

Lupita: I'll try. Shall I call the airline office?

Igor: That's great. I could probably do it, but my Spanish is a little rusty.

Lupita: So what room are you in?

Igor: Let's see ... 103.

Lupita: OK. I'll call you back later.

Igor: Thanks, Lupita. How about dinner tonight?

Lupita: Sounds good. Bye.

M. Check the Internet:

<www.tourbymexico.com/yucatan/chichen/chichen.htm>

The Grand Canyon
Arizona, USA

26

It's a grand Canyon!

PHOTOGRAPHER: © LORPIC 99 | AGENCY: DREAMSTIME.COM

WHAT? the Grand Canyon

WHERE? Arizona

HOW LONG? 227 miles

HOW DEEP? one mile

HOW WIDE? 18 miles

WHO? artists and tourists

WHAT? the Colorado River

WHERE? at the bottom

A. Where's Igor?

(rrrrring)

Igor:	He-he-llooh.
You:	Igor? Did I wake you up?
Igor:	Yeah, you did. That's OK.
You:	Well, where are you?
Igor:	Arizona.
You:	Really? In Arizona? How did you get there?
Igor:	Three days on a bus from Mexico.
You:	What are doing there?
Igor:	Right now I'm resting up for tomorrow.
You:	What are you going to do tomorrow?
Igor:	I'm going to the bottom of the Grand Canyon!
You:	Wow! Be careful, but have fun!
Igor:	I'll be careful, and I'll have fun ... if I can get some rest.
You:	OK. Bye.

B. Do you know these words?

deep _____

wide _____

a side _____

majestic_____

to ride _____

a mule_____

an expedition _____

a raft _____

C. Read.

The Grand Canyon is huge. It is 227 miles long and one mile deep. In its widest place it is 18 miles wide from one side to the other. The Canyon is majestic and beautiful. It has different colors throughout the day — pink, red, purple, and brown. Artists come to paint it. Tourists come to look, camp, and hike. They can ride a mule from the top to the bottom of the Canyon. They can see two billion years of earth's history in the rock walls of the Canyon.

The Colorado River is at the bottom of the Canyon. In 1869 an expedition on boats traveled through the entire Canyon. They were the first people to do that. Nowadays many tourism companies offer rafting expeditions on the river. Whatever you do at the Canyon, you will never forget it. (140)

D. Answer: *I agree with that.* **or** *I don't agree with that.*

1. The Grand Canyon is a river. _____

2. The Grand Canyon is not small. _____

3. It's 18 miles deep. _____

4. The Grand Canyon is in California. _____

5. Mules hike in the Grand Canyon. _____

6. The Colorado River is in Arizona. _____

7. You cannot use rafts on the river. _____

E. Write the answers.

1. What is the Grand Canyon? _____

2. Where is the Grand Canyon? _____

3. How long is the Canyon? _____

4. Who comes to the Canyon? _____

5. Why do they come to the Canyon? _____

F. Grammar check. Use prepositions: *in* or *at* or *on*.

1. The river is _____ the bottom.

2. I want to go _____ the afternoon.

3. Let's go _____ three o'clock.

4. Let's go _____ Monday.

5. I want to go _____ the evening.

6. I want to go _____ night.

7. I want to go _____ the summer.

8. You can ride _____ a mule.

9. You can raft _____ the river.

G. Word check. Fill in the blanks.

Use: *long, deep, wide, side, majestic, ride, mule, bottom, expedition, raft*

1. The Grand Canyon is beautiful and _____.

2. It is very _____, _____, and _____.

3. It is very wide from one _____ to another.

4. You can _____ on a _____.

5. You can _____ on the river.

6. An _____ traveled the river in 1869.

7. A river is at the _____ of the Canyon.

H. Listen and write.

1. _____

2. _____

3. _____

4. _____

5. _____

Where in the World...

I. Writing check.

Write a postcard to a friend about the Grand Canyon.

Come to the Canyon!

Navajo weaving   USA37

J. Pronunciation check.

Did you ever see
Anything wider?
Anything greater?
No! No! Never, ever!
It's a grand place
to ride a raft,
It's a must-see place,
a must-do place,
For all to see,
For all to see.

anything bigger?
Anything longer?
Anything grander?
Never, ever! No! No!
to ride a mule,
to take a hike.
a must-go place,
a must see-go-do place.
to look and see,
Go, look, do, see!

K. Talk about it in small groups.

Would you like to see the Grand Canyon? Why?
What would you do here?
How long would you stay?

L. It's Igor.

(rrrrring)

Igor: Hello?

Laura: Where in the world have you been?

Igor: Oh, hi, Laura. Arizona.

Laura: I was worried. Was your phone off?

Igor: No. I was in a big hole.

Laura: What!

Igor: Yeah. I was riding a mule.

Laura: And you fell into a hole?

Igor: Actually I was at the bottom of the Grand Canyon.

Laura: Igooor!

Igor: Anyway, I'm back at the top, and I'll call you tonight.

Laura: All right. Talk to you later.

M. Check the Internet: <www.nps.gov/goga>

27

PHOTOGRAPHER: © JEREMY BRUSKOTTER | AGENCY: DREAMSTIME.COM

WHAT? peninsulas

WHAT? strait

WHAT? bridge

WHAT KIND? suspension

WHAT? park

WHAT? forest

WHAT? prison

HOW MANY? two

HOW WIDE? narrow

HOW LONG? 1.7 miles

WHAT KIND? urban

WHERE? Muir Woods

WHERE? Alcatraz

A. Where's Igor?

(rrrrring)

Igor:	**Hello!**
You:	**Hello! Igor? Where are you?**
Igor:	**I'm suspended in air.**
You:	**What! Are you in a hot air balloon?**
Igor:	**No, I'm walking across the Golden Gate Bridge.**
You:	**How's the view from there?**
Igor:	**Spectacular! The bay, the ocean, hills, boats, ships, Alcatraz, and the great city of San Francisco.**
You:	**That sounds wonderful.**
Igor:	**It is. I wish you were here.**
You:	**Thanks. Maybe some day. So take care.**
Igor:	**Talk to you later.**

B. Do you know these words?

gate _____

narrow _____

between _____

bay _____

bridge _____

urban _____

park _____

infamous _____

prison _____

C. Read.

California's Golden Gate is on the Pacific coast. The Golden Gate is like a door. At the gate there is a narrow strait between two peninsulas. On one side of the gate is the Pacific Ocean. On the other side is San Francisco Bay.

The Golden Gate Bridge connects two peninsulas. It is a beautiful suspension bridge. It is over one mile long. It has two orange towers that are 746 feet tall. Thousands of cars cross the bridge every day. People love to walk across the bridge. Some ride their bicycles. They love the view from the bridge.

The bridge is part of an urban park. It brings parks to the people. Golden Gate National Recreation Area includes 59 miles of coastline. It also includes the great redwood trees of Muir Woods. On an island in the bay is the infamous prison called Alcatraz. It is now a museum. (150)

D. Answer. Write: *That's true.* or *That's false.*

1. The Golden Gate Bridge is beautiful. _____

2. It is in Alcatraz. _____

3. People like to walk across it. _____

4. The Golden Gate Bridge is 746 feet long. _____

5. A recreation area is like a park. _____

6. People cannot ride a bicycle across the bridge. _____

7. You can see San Francisco from the bridge. _____

8. Muir Woods is on an island. _____

E. Write the answers.

1. What is Golden Gate Recreation Area? _____

2. Where is it? _____

3. How long is the Golden Gate Bridge? _____

4. Why do people walk across the bridge? _____

5. What is Alcatraz? _____

F. Grammar check. Use pronouns: I, You, He, She, It, We, You, They

Example: *Igor and Maria* are in Arizona. *They are in Arizona.*

1. *Mary* is going to San Francisco. _____

2. *John* is going with her. _____

3. *Mary and John* are going. _____

4. *Mary and I* are tourists. _____

5. *The Bridge* is beautiful. _____

6. Are *you and John* on the bridge? _____

7. Are you at Alcatraz, *John*? Yes, _____ am.

G. Word check. Fill in the blanks. Use: *gate, narrow, between, bay, bridge, urban, park, infamous, prison*

1. Alcatraz was a _____.

2. There is a _____ strait _____ the two peninsulas.

3. The island is in the middle of the _____.

4. The longest suspension _____ is in Japan.

5. There are many trees in this _____.

6. The park's front _____ opens at 7 a.m.

7. Cities are _____ areas.

8. Alcatraz was not a nice place; it was _____.

H. Listen and write.

1. _____

2. _____

3. _____

4. _____

5. _____

I. Writing check.

Write a postcard to a friend about Golden Gate National Recreation Area.

*seeing the sights
in San Francisco*

29
USA   *Daffodil*

_____

_____

_____

_____

J. Pronunciation check.

Tell me about
the very, very famous
In San Francisco?
In California?
Can we walk it?
Can we bike it?
That's the plan!
That's in the plan.

the famous bridge,
Golden Gate Bridge.
Yes, indeed!
Right, again!
Yes, we can!
That's the plan!
And Alcatraz?
Great! Let's go!

K. Talk about it in small groups.

What do you do for recreation?

Why do some people love bridges?

What's interesting about a bridge?

Do you know about other famous bridges?

L. It's Igor.

(rrrrring)

Lee: Hello?

Igor: Hello, Lee. I want to say thanks again for a great weekend.

Lee: It was fun, wasn't it?

Igor: Lunch in Chinatown was great.

Lee: How about dinner at Fisherman's Wharf?

Igor: Wonderful!

Lee: Muir Woods?

Igor: Beautiful!

Lee: Alcatraz?

Igor: Fascinating.

Lee: The baseball game?

Igor: Fun! So how can I pay you back?

Lee: I'll be in Boston in September.

Igor: Great! What do you want to see?

Lee: Fenway Park.

Igor: You're on! See you in September.

M. Check the Internet: <www.nps.gov/goga>

28

Old Faithful Geyser

WHAT? a national park

WHERE? Wyoming

WHEN? 1872

HOW MANY? 64 parks
390 sites

WHY? to camp, hike, fish, see animals

A. Where's Igor?

(rrrrring)

Igor:	Hello!
You:	Hello, Igor. Where are you?
Igor:	I'm at a national park.
You:	Really? Which one? Yosemite?
Igor:	Nope. But it begins with a Y.
You:	Aha! Yellowstone!
Igor:	Right.
You:	What are you doing there?
Igor:	Hiking and fishing and looking at the geysers.
You:	How about animals? Have you seen many?
Igor:	You name it, I've seen it.
You:	Which ones are the most interesting?
Igor:	Hmmm. I like the bisons.
You:	The strangest?
Igor:	No question: homo sapiens.
You:	OK, Igor. Give me a call when you leave.
Igor:	Bye.

B. Do you know these words?

to manage _____

a seashore _____

a site _____

an acre _____

a forest _____

a lake _____

a geyser _____

to fish _____

to enjoy _____

outdoors _____

overcrowded _____

a snowmobile _____

a limit _____

C. Read.

Yellowstone National Park is the oldest national park in the United States. It became a national park in 1872. It is one of 64 national parks. The parks are managed by the National Park Service. The service manages 390 places. In addition to the national parks, other places are national monuments, seashores, recreation areas, and historical sites.

Yellowstone is mostly in Wyoming. A few acres of the park are in Montana and Idaho. Yellowstone has beautiful mountains, forests, and lakes. It has incredible geysers, too. You can camp, hike, fish, and see many animals there. Over a million people visit Yellowstone all year to enjoy the great outdoors.

National parks are for everyone to enjoy. However, a popular park like Yellowstone can be overcrowded in the summer. In the winter too many people want to ride snowmobiles in the park. Now there is a limit on how many may use the park each day. (154)

D. Answer: *That's true.* or *That isn't true.*

1. There are 390 national parks. _____

2. Yellowstone is in only one state. _____

3. Yellowstone has a beautiful seashore. _____

4. A geyser is an animal. _____

5. People can go fishing in Yellowstone. _____

6. You cannot hike in Yellowstone. _____

7. There are many animals in Yellowstone. _____

E. Write the answers.

1. What is Yellowstone? _____

2. Where is Yellowstone? _____

3. Who goes there? _____

4. Why do they go there? _____

5. When do they go? _____

F. Grammar check. Use *that* or *those*.

1. Look at _____ geyser.

2. Did _____ hiker climb _____ mountains?

3. Look at all _____ animals.

4. _____ mountain is very tall.

5. _____ fish are really big.

6. Are _____ campers from Canada?

7. Can we climb _____ mountains?

8. _____ is a beautiful view!

G. Word check. Fill in the blanks. Use: *manages, seashore, sites, acres, forest, lake, fish, enjoy, outdoors, overcrowded, snowmobiles*

1. There are too many people here. It's _____.

2. Some parks are thousands of _____ in size.

3. The Park Service _____ many _____.

4. I _____ the park all year. It's great to be _____ .

5. There are lots of _____ in this _____.

6. People ride _____ in the winter.

7. Do you prefer to swim at the lake or at the _____?

8. There are millions of trees in this _____ .

H. Listen and write.

1. _____

2. _____

3. _____

4. _____

5. _____

I. Writing check.

Write a postcard to a friend about Yellowstone.

Postcard

_____

_____

_____

_____

Come and See the Living Wilderness

J. Pronunciation check.

Do you want to fish?	Yes, I do; yes, I do!
Do you want to hike?	Yes, I do; yes, I do!
See some geysers?	Yes, I do; yes, I do!
Lots of animals?	Of course I do!
Then Yellowstone is	the place for you!
Yellowstone is	the place for you!

K. Talk about it.

Do you like the outdoors?
What do you like to do there?
Have you been to any national parks?

L. It's Igor.

(rrrrring)

Igor: **Hello.**

Dad: **Hello Igor. Where are you?**

Igor: **Oh, hi, Dad! I'm in Canada.**

Dad: **Canada? I thought you were in Wyoming.**

Igor: **Yeah, I was, and the hiking in Yellowstone was great.**

Dad: **So how did you get to Canada?**

Igor: **I got a ride with another hiker and then took the bus.**

Dad: **What's that sound?**

Igor: **I'm on a train.**

Dad: **Where are you going?**

Igor: **Across Canada to Toronto. Here comes my dinner!**
            Say hello to Mom.

Dad: **OK. See you soon, I hope.**

M. Check the Internet: < www.nps.gov/yell>

Niagara Falls
New York, USA, and Ontario, Canada

29

falling in love with Niagara Falls

WHAT? an inland waterway, waterfalls

WHERE? between the U.S. and Canada, on the Niagara River

WHO? tourists, honeymooners, daredevils

WHY? big, beautiful, loud

A. Where's Igor?

(rrrrring)
You: Hello, Igor? Where are you?
Igor: I'm at Niagara Falls.
You: Niagara Falls?
Igor: Yes, I'm on my honeymoon!
You: Really? You just got married?
Igor: Last week.
You: No way! You're pulling my leg.
Igor: Yeah. Just kidding. I'm actually on the last leg of my trip.
You: So when do you get home?
Igor: Soon. I'll call when I get there.
You: Great! I can't wait to hear all about your adventures.
Igor: Talk to you later. Take care.

B. Do you know these words?

to share_____

inland _____

a waterway _____

halfway _____

waterfalls_____

loud_____

to light_____

a honeymoon _____

a daredevil _____

(to) survive _____

barrel_____

electricity_____

C. Read.

The United States and Canada share a very important inland waterway that flows from the Great Lakes to the Atlantic Ocean. The Niagara River connects the two eastern lakes, Lake Erie and Lake Ontario. About halfway between the two lakes is Niagara Falls, on the Niagara River.

Niagara Falls is, in fact, three waterfalls between the United States and Canada. On one side is the state of New York. On the other is the province of Ontario. The falls are big, beautiful, and very loud! At night they are lighted with colored lights. It's a very popular place for honeymoons. It is also a popular place for daredevils. In 1829 a man went over the falls and survived. In 1901 a woman went over the falls in a barrel. She also survived. But many have died.

Niagara Falls is a famous recreational and tourism area. The falls are also important because they make electricity for the United States and Canada. (160)

D. Answer: *Yes, that's quite true.* or *That's not true at all.*

1. Niagara Falls is between the U.S. and Canada._____

2. The falls are on the Ontario River. _____

3. A honeymoon is a kind of trip._____

4. Honeymooners are daredevils._____

5. Niagara Falls is beautiful at night._____

6. Lake Ontario is one of the Great Lakes._____

7. The falls are between Toronto and Erie. _____

8. The falls also make electricity. _____

E. Write the answers.

1. What is Niagara Falls? _____

2. Where is Niagara Falls? _____

3. Who goes there? _____

4. Why do people go there? _____

5. What do the falls make? _____

Niagara Falls

F. Grammar check. Change to contractions.

Example: *We are in Canada.* > *We're* in Canada.

1. I am a student. _____ a student.

2. He is a teacher. _____ a teacher.

3. We are tourists. _____ tourists.

4. They are on their honeymoon. _____ on their honeymoon.

5. You are from China. _____ from China.

6. She is at Niagara Falls. _____ at Niagara Falls.

7. Mary is in New York. _____ in New York.

G. Word check. Fill in the blanks. Use: *share, inland waterway, halfway, loud, lights, honeymooners, Daredevils, survived, barrel, electricity*

1. Niagara Falls are on an _____ between the United States and Canada. The two countries _____ the falls.

2. People who just got married are _____.

3. A young boy _____ going over the falls.

4. _____ try to go over the falls in a _____.

5. The falls make _____ for Canada and the United States.

6. The falls are _____. You can hear their sound from far away.

7. At night, there are colored _____ on the falls.

8. We traveled _____ across Canada.

H. Listen and write.

1. _____

2. _____

3. _____

4. _____

5. _____

Where in the World...

I. Writing check.

Write a postcard to a friend about Niagara Falls.

```
POSTCARD        CARTE POSTALE                    $1  CANADA




                                           _____

                                           _____

                                           _____

                                           _____
```

J. Pronunciation check.

Where are they going?   To Niagara Falls.
Why are they going   to see the falls?
Where are they staying?   The honeymoon suite.
They just got married?   Didn't you know?
No, I didn't.   So now you know.
Do you want to go?   I don't know.
I'll go if you go.   I'll go with the flow.

K. Talk about it.

Do you like waterfalls? Why or why not?

Have you seen one? Where?

Where do people in your family go after they get married?

L. It's Igor.

Clerk: Thank you for calling Motel D.C. Can I help you?

Igor: Yes. I'd like to make a reservation.

Clerk: What nights, please?

Igor: This Saturday through Monday.

Clerk: OK. Single or double?

Igor: Single, please.

Clerk: Do you want to hold the room with a credit card?

Igor: No, thanks.

Clerk: Then we'll hold the room until 6 p.m.

Igor: That's good. What's the rate?

Clerk: Two oh nine ninety-five plus tax.

Igor: Hmm. Nothing cheaper?

Clerk: I'm afraid not, sir.

Igor: OK. I'll try someplace else. Bye.

M. Check the Internet: <en.wikipedia.org/wiki/Niagara_Falls>

WHAT? the National Mall   WHERE? Washington, D.C.

WHAT? memorials, monuments, museums

WHERE? on the Mall

WHO? senators and representatives

WHERE? the Capitol Building

A. Where's Igor?

(rrrrring)

Igor: Hello!

You: Hello, Igor. Where are you today?

Igor: I'm at the Mall.

You: You're shopping?

Igor: No, I'm walking along our National Mall.

You: Oh, so you're in Washington, D.C.

Igor: Right you are! And this place is inspiring.

You: Yeah it is, isn't it?

Igor: I am really inspired. Everyone should come here.

You: I saw it in April. It was beautiful. All the cherry trees were covered with flowers.

Igor: Thanks to Japan for that great gift.

You: Right. Igor, call me on Wednesday, will you?

Igor: Sure thing. Bye bye.

B. Do you know these words?

an end_____

a mall _____

a landmark _____

a monument _____

along_____

Congress _____

to meet _____

a law _____

to look around _____

a speech _____

C. Read.

The National Mall is a long, narrow park. From one end to the other it has many of Washington's famous landmarks. At one end is the Lincoln Memorial. Lincoln looks down the mall to the Capitol Building at the other end. If you walk from the Lincoln Memorial to the Capitol, you can see memorials for the Vietnam War, the Korean War, and World War II. The tall Washington Monument is partway down the Mall. From there you can see the White House. Along the sides of the Mall are some of America's greatest museums.

The Capitol Building is a very important, famous, and beautiful building. The Capitol was built in 1793. It is where Congress meets. Congress includes 100 senators and 435 representatives of the American people. They make laws for the U.S. Today tourists can walk inside the Capitol Building and look around. They can listen to speeches.

Not far from the Capitol Building is the Supreme Court, and on top of the Capitol Building is the Statue of Freedom. (174)

D. Answer.

1. Is the Capitol Building on the Mall? _____

2. Are there only two war memorials?_____

3. Does Congress make laws for the country?_____

4. Is the Capitol in the state of Washington? _____

5. Is the Statue of Liberty on top of the Capitol? _____

6. Does Congress work in the White House? _____

E. Write the answers.

1. What is the National Mall? _____

2. Where is the Capitol Building? _____

3. When was the building built? _____

4. Who works there?_____

5. Why does Congress meet there? _____

Washington, D.C.

F. Grammar check. Circle the correct word in the blank.

Example: The President lives ((in,) to) the White House.

1. (From, At) one end to another there are many museums.

2. The Capitol is (at, from) one end of the Mall.

3. The Washington Monument is (on, to) the Mall.

4. Congress makes laws (for, to) the people.

5. (Along, From) the sides are three war memorials.

6. Not far (to, from) the Capitol Building is the Supreme Court.

7. On (top, top of) the building is a statue.

8. You can walk (at, inside) the Capitol and look around.

G. Word check. Fill in the blanks. Use: *end, Mall, landmark, Monument, Along, Congress, meets, laws, look around, speeches*

1. Congress makes _____ for all the people.

2. _____ works in the Capitol Building.

3. The Washington _____ is a famous _____.

4. _____ the Mall there are many famous places.

5. The senate _____ in the Capitol.

6. At one _____ of the Mall is the Lincoln Memorial.

7. The _____ is a long narrow park.

8. Inside, you can _____ and listen to _____.

H. Listen and write.

1. _____

2. _____

3. _____

4. _____

5. _____

Where in the World...

I. Writing check.

Write a postcard to a friend about Washington, D.C.

GREETINGS
FROM THE NATION'S CAPITAL

PHOTOGRAPHER: © GEOPAPPAS | AGENCY: DREAMSTIME.COM

J. Pronunciation check.

Washington,	Washington,
Washington,	D.C.
has many buildings	that you must see!
The Capitol's big,	with a rounded dome
for the U.S. Congress.	It is their home.
The Capitol Building	we all must see.
It's very important	for democracy!

K. Talk about Washington, D.C.

Would you like to visit Washington, D.C.?

What would like to see?

Have you visited any important government buildings?

Where are they? What did you see?

L. It's Igor.

(rrrrring)

Mom: Hello?

Igor: Hi, Mom!

Mom: Igor, where are you? At South Station, I hope.

Igor: No, I'm at Union Station.

Mom: You're still in Washington?

Igor: Yeah, I just couldn't leave without seeing the National Air and Space Museum.

Mom: But you'll be home soon, won't you?

Igor: The day after tomorrow.

Mom: It will be so good to see you. We've missed you so much.

Igor: Same here, Mom. It'll be good to be home again. Say hello to Dad. See you soon. Bye.

M. Check the Internet: <www.nps.gov/nama

Word List

The number indicates the lesson number in which the word first appears.

about	19	(to) build	2	(to) cover	20
accident	24	(to) bury	13	crater	7
accurate	25	busy	8	cultural	12
acre	28	(to) buy	8	culture	22
active	18	calendar	25	czar	9
air	11	(to) camp	18	(to) damage	5
ancient	6	capital	16	dangerous	11
anthropologist	7	carving	16	daredevil	29
approximately	19	cathedral	5	dark	20
along	30	cattle	21	deep	26
architect	3	(to) celebrate	9	dense	21
army	13	center	8	(to) depend on	19
artist	3	century	5	descendant	25
(to) attract	22	ceremony	22	(to) design	3
(to) bake	13	church	3	(to) develop	23
barrel	29	clay	13	(to) die	10
bay	27	(to) clear	21	(to) dive	17
beautiful	1	(to) climb	2	dome	3
behind	6	close	22	dream	24
(to) belong to	19	coast	17	dry	20
between	4	cold	20	early man	7
body	6	colorful	17	earth	21
bones	7	(to) come up	15	earthquake	5
border	11	(to) complete	24	economic	12
(to) bother	23	complex	25	electricity	29
bottom	26	cone	15	emperor	10
(to) breathe	11	(to) connect	24	end	30
bridge	27	construction	24	enemy(ies)	4
(to) bubble	18	continent	20	(to) enjoy	28
Buddhist	12	coral	17	(to) establish	25

evolution	23	(to) grow	21	law	30
exile	12	(to) guard	4	leader	12
expedition	26	guide	11	(to) leave	18
expensive	24	halfway	29	liberty	1
explorer	20	harbor	1	life-size	13
(to) fail	24	health	21	(to) light	29
(a) fair	2	(to) hike	18	limit	28
fantastic	17	high	4	lion	6
famous	2	hill	4	lizard	23
farmer	21	Hindu	16	logger	21
fast	21	historical	9	long	6
(to) fight	13	history	16	(to) look around	30
(to) find	7	(to) hold	3	lost	22
(to) finish	14	honeymoon	29	loud	29
fire	5	(to) honor	4	lungs	21
(to) fish	28	hope	1	majestic	26
flag	16	horse	13	malaria	24
(to) flow	18	huge	6	mall	30
(to) fly	23	ice sheet	20	(to) manage	28
forest	28	including	9	marble	10
forever	10	incredible	10	(to) meet	30
(to) form	17	infamous	27	memorial	10
freedom	1	inland	29	monument	30
(to) freeze	20	insane	9	moon	14
fresh	15	island	17	mosaics	5
game preserve	7	isolated	19	mosque	5
garden	10	jewels	12	mountain	8
gate	27	(to) kill	9	museum	5
gem	10	king	6	mystery	19
geyser	28	kingdom	16	narrow	27
gift	18	lake	28	near	23
gold	5	landmark	30	others	19
goods	8	lava	18	outdoors	28

overcrowded	28	(to) save	24	threat	23
overnight	15	sea	14	tiny	17
painting(s)	3	seal	20	tomb	8
palace	12	seashore	28	top	2
park	7	(to) sell	8	tower	2
penguin	20	(to) share	29	(to) trade	8
peninsula	25	shell	17	tribe	8
perhaps	22	(to) shrink	21	trip	15
place	22	side	26	underground	13
planet	21	site	28	unique	23
political	12	skillful	25	unusual	8
popular	22	sky	22	(to) use	24
powerful	23	snowmobile	28	victory	9
(to) pray	18	snowstorm	11	volcano	7
present	1	soldier	13	view	2
prison	27	speech	30	wall	14
(to) protect	4	(to) stand	8	warrior	13
proud	16	statue	1	(to) watch	15
province	4	(to) stay	15	waterfalls	29
public	18	stone	16	waterway	29
pyramid	6	story	16	way	14
raft	26	strange	19	weather	11
reef	17	structure	2	(to) weigh	23
religious	12	surface	17	west	14
(to) remain	17	(to) surround	20	wide	26
(to) remember	10	(to) survive	29	wildlife	7
the rest	19	(to) swim	17	(to) wind	14
(to) ride	26	symbol	1	windy	20
river	10	system	25	wonderful	2
rock	26	tall	1	wood	21
ruin(s)	4	temple	4	worker	6
sacred	15	terrible	9	world	1
safari	7	thin	11		

Dictations

1. The Statue of Liberty - page 1 (Optional Dictations CD 1: track 1)

1. I like   New York   and France.
2. Is   the statue   in New York?
3. The statue   is very tall,   isn't she?
4. She came   to New York   in 1884.
5. Lady Liberty   is another name   for the statue.

2. The Eiffel Tower - page 7 (Dictations CD 1: track 2)

1. It is   a very tall   structure.
2. You   can see   all of Paris.
3. The World's Fair   was   in 1889.
4. The city of Paris   is   very beautiful.
5. Eiffel   built the tower   and   the Statue of Liberty.

3. St. Peter's Cathedral - page 13 (Dictations CD 1: track 3)

1. Vatican City   is in the city   of Rome.
2. It is   the largest church   in the world.
3. The church   was begun   a long time ago.   *Is very old*
4. Michelangelo was   an artist   and an architect.
5. Many famous artists   made paintings   for the Vatican.

4. The Parthenon - page 19 (Dictations CD 1: track 4)

1. Is   the temple   on a hill?
2. Can you see   all of   Athens?
3. Are there   many ruins   in Greece?
4. Was the temple   built   a long time ago?
5. Did the Greeks   have   many enemies?

5. Ayasofya - page 25 (Dictations CD 1: track 5)

1. The city of Istanbul   is in Europe.
2. Ayasofya was   a cathedral,   and a mosque.
3. Earthquakes   often damaged   the building.
4. The country of Turkey   is in Europe   and in Asia.
5. Atatürk was   the president   of Turkey.

Where in the World...

6. The Great Sphinx - page 31 (Dictations CD 1: track 6)

1. Where is   the Great Sphinx?
2. The huge statue   is very long.
3. When was   the Sphinx   built?
4. Does anybody know   why the sphinx   was built?
5. Why does   the Sphinx   have the body   of a lion?

[handwritten notes: Worker build the Sphinx / = Why was te sphin bit / The sphinx is / ancient]

7. Ngorongoro Game Preserve - page 37 (Dictations CD 1: track 7)

1. Many animals   come and go   in the crater.
2. Many tourists   come to see   the wild animals.
3. The wildlife park   is   in Tanzania, Africa.
4. The preserve   is   in a crater   of an old volcano.
5. The bones   of early man   were found   near the park.

8. Petra - page 43 (Dictations CD 1: track 8)

1. Are the buildings   red in color?
2. Was it   a busy   trading center?
3. Is Petra   an ancient city   in Jordan?
4. Are some temples   in the side   of a mountain?
5. Are the temples   and tombs   really famous?

9. St. Basil's Cathedral - page 49 (Dictations CD 1: track 9)

1. Today   many people   visit   Red Square.
2. Is the Kremlin   near   St. Basil's cathedral?
3. Ivan the Terrible   was not   a good czar.
4. He built   the cathedral   to celebrate   a victory.
5. Are the cathedral   and Red Square   in Moscow?

10. The Taj Mahal - page 55 (Dictations CD 1: track 10)

1. The Taj Mahal   is   a beautiful tomb.
2. It   was made   with white marble.
3. It is   a memorial   to his wife.
4. He was   the emperor   of India.
5. There are   many gems   on the floor.

Dictations   **185**

11. Mount Everest - page 61 (Dictations CD 1: track 11)

1. The air   is very thin   on the top.
2. Mount Everest   is   the tallest mountain.
3. It is   a very dangerous   mountain.
4. Many people   have tried   to climb it.
5. The first men   to climb it   did it   in 1953.

12. Potala Palace - page 67 (Dictations CD 1: track 12)

1. Today,   the palace   is a museum.
2. The palace   is   the Dalai Lama's home.
3. There are   over 1000 rooms   in the palace.
4. The palace   was built   in the seventh century.
5. The Dalai Lama   is living   in exile   in India.

13. The Terra Cotta Warriors - page 73 (Dictations CD 1: track 13)

1. The warriors   are   life-size statues.
2. They   were found   in 1974.
3. They   are made   of baked clay.
4. They guard   the tomb   of an emperor.
5. It is   one   of the oldest cities   in the world.

14. The Great Wall - page 79 (Dictations CD 1: track 14)

1. Thousands   of workers   built the wall.
2. It took   many centuries   to build it.
3. You   can see it   from space.
4. The wall   winds from the west   to the sea.
5. Today, tourists   come to see and   walk on the wall.

15. Mount Fuji - page 85 (Dictations CD 1: track 15)

1. Is it   the tallest mountain   in Japan?
2. Do you think   Mount Fuji   is an old volcano?
3. Is summer   the best time   to climb Fuji?
4. Can people   stay overnight   on the top?
5. Do they   watch the sun   come up   in the morning?

Where in the World...

16. Angkor Wat - page 91 (Optional Dictations CD 2: track 1)

1. Angkor was   the capital city   of the kingdom.
2. The temples have   many wonderful carvings.
3. Angkor Wat is   an unusually   large temple.
4. There is   a picture   of Angkor Wat   on the flag.
5. The people   of Cambodia   are proud   of the temple.

17. The Great Barrier Reef - page 97 (Dictations CD 2: track 2)

1. These tiny animals   make   limestone shells.
2. They formed   the longest reef   in the world.
3. The reef   is along   the northeast coast   of Australia.
4. Australians and tourists   like to swim   and dive   at the reef.
5. The coral   has   many beautiful colors   and unusual forms.

18. Hawaii Volcanoes National Park - page 103 (Dictations CD 2: track 3)

1. The national park   is   an unusual place.
2. Many Hawaiians   believe   Pele lives there.
3. You   can actually see   the red-hot lava.
4. They   leave gifts   and pray   to keep her quiet.
5. The park   is very large   and you   can hike   and camp there.

19. Easter Island - page 109 (Dictations CD 2: track 4)

1. Easter Island   is   a small, isolated island.
2. There are   about 887 statues   on the island.
3. Today   about 3,500 people   live on the island.
4. It is 2,237 miles   from the Chilean coast.
5. Some people   think   they were made   about 440 C.E.

20. Antarctica - page 115 (Dictations CD 2: track 5)

1. Antarctica   is covered   by an ice sheet.
2. It is actually   the driest place   in the world.
3. Some explorers   froze to death   on Antarctica.
4. It is   a high continent,   surrounded by   icy waters.
5. Antarctica is   a windy,   cold, and dark   continent.

21. The Amazon Rainforest - page 121 (Dictations CD 2: track 6)
1. The rainforest   is the biggest   on earth.
2. People   are cutting   the trees   for wood.
3. The trees and plants   are   very close together.
4. Rainforests   are the lungs   of our planet.
5. The Amazon Rainforest   is getting   smaller and smaller.

22. Machu Picchu - page 127 (Dictations CD 2: track 7)
1. There is   an ancient city   in the Andes.
2. The Inca Indians   built it   a long time ago.
3. Perhaps they thought   gods lived   in the sky.
4. Maybe it was   a special place   for ceremonies.
5. Today tourists come   from all around   the world.

23. The Galapagos Islands - page 133 (Dictations CD 2: track 8)
1. The islands are   600 miles   from Ecuador.
2. There are many   strange and unique   animals there.
3. Some of   the tortoises   weigh   over 500 pounds.
4. Many tourists   visit the islands   every year   to see the wildlife.
5. Too many tourists   can be   a threat   to the animals.

24. The Panama Canal - page 139 (Dictations CD 2: track 9)
1. The Panama canal   connects   two oceans.
2. The canal is   just over   50 miles long.
3. First the French   tried in 1880   but they failed.
4. Thousands of workers   died from accidents   and malaria.
5. A ship   can save   over 7,000 miles   and many days   by using the canal.

25. Chichen Itza - page 145 (Dictations CD 2: track 10)
1. Chichen Itza is   a very old   Mayan city.
2. It was established   on the Yucatán Peninsula   in 514 C.E.
3. The Maya developed   a complex   writing system.
4. The pyramid was   probably used   for many   different ceremonies.
5. How did the Maya   design and build   these places   so many years ago?

26. The Grand Canyon - page 151 (Dictations CD 2: track 11)

1. The Grand Canyon   is 227 miles   long.
2. Tourists can ride   a mule   at the Canyon.
3. The Colorado River   is at the bottom   of the Canyon.
4. Tourism companies   offer many expeditions   at the Canyon.
5. There is   a lot of history   in the canyon's   rocks and walls.

27. Golden Gate National Recreation Area (Dictations CD 2: track 12)

1. The Golden Gate   is like   a door.
2. There is   a narrow strait   between   the peninsulas.
3. The prison is   on an island   in the middle   of the bay.
4. Many people   cross the bridge   on bicycles   every day.
5. The park   also includes   the redwood trees   of beautiful   Muir Woods.

28. Yellowstone National Park - page 163 (Dictations CD 2: track 13)

1. Yellowstone is   the oldest   national park.
2. The National Park Service   manages   many places.
3. Over a million people   visit Yellowstone   every year.
4. Popular parks   can be   very overcrowded   in the summer.
5. Now there is   a limit   on the number   who can visit every day.

29. Niagara Falls - page 169 (Dictations CD 2: track 14)

1. The United States   and Canada   share   the falls.
2. It is   a popular place   for honeymoons.
3. Some daredevils   went over the falls   and survived.
4. In fact,   there are   three waterfalls   on the river.
5. The falls   are also important   because they make   electricity.

30. Washington, D.C. - page 175 (Dictations CD 2: track 15)

1. The National Mall is   a long, narrow park.
2. At one end   of the Mall   is the Lincoln Memorial.
3. The senators   and representatives   make laws   for the country.
4. The Capitol Building is   very important,   famous, and beautiful.
5. You can walk inside   and look around   and listen   to speeches.

Answers

1. The Statue of Liberty - page 1

D. 1. Yes, it is.
2. No, it isn't.
3. No, it isn't.
4. Yes, it is.
5. Yes, it is.

F. 1. It
2. her
3. them
4. him
5. them
6. us
7. me
8. you

G. 1. Liberty, freedom
2. Harbor
3. statues
4. tall, beautiful
5. present
6. symbol
7. hope

2. The Eiffel Tower - page 7

D. 1. No, it isn't.
2. No, it isn't.
3. Yes, it is.
4. No, it wasn't.
5. Yes, it is.
6. Yes, it was.
7. No, it isn't.
8. Yes, it was.

F. 1. want
2. wants
3. wants
4. want
5. want
6. want
7. want
8. wants
9. wants

G. 1. tower (structure)
2. Fair
3. built
4. famous
5. wonderful, view
6. climb, top
7. structure (tower)

3. Saint Peter's Cathedral - page 13

D. 1. I don't agree.
2. I agree.
3. I don't agree.
4. I don't agree.
5. I agree.
6. I don't agree.
7. I agree.

F. 1. St. Peter's church
2. Michelangelo's dome
3. Rome's famous places
4. a friend's post card
5. Italy's churches
6. an artist's work
7. the building's architect
8. the statues's designer

G. 1. designed
2. holds
3. dome
4. architect
5. artists, paintings
6. church

4. The Parthenon - page 19

D. 1. That's right.
2. That's right.
3. That's wrong.
4. That's wrong.
5. That's right.
6. That's wrong.
7. That's right.
8. That's wrong.

F. 1. The Greeks loved Athena.
   2. The Greeks honored Athena.
   3. Athena guarded the city.
   4. She protected the city.
   5. We looked a the Temple.
   6. They climbed the hill.
   7. We asked many questions.

G. 1. honor
   2. ruins
   3. high
   4. Temple
   5. between
   6. guarded, protected
   7. enemies
   8. hill

5. Ayasofya - page 25

D. 1. No, that's incorrect.
   2. Yes, that's correct.
   3. Yes, that's correct.
   4. Yes, that's correct.
   5. No, that's incorrect.
   6. Yes, that's correct.
   7. No, that's incorrect.
   8. No, that's incorrect.

F. 1. We didn't go to Iran.
   2. She didn't see Romania.
   3. I didn't buy postcards.
   4. He didn't take many pictures.
   5. I didn't eat Greek food.
   6. You didn't sleep well on the plane.
   7. They didn't spend a lot of money.

G. 1. damaged
   2. century
   3. museum
   4. mosaics
   5. Earthquakes, fire
   6. gold
   7. cathedral
   8. mosque

6. The Great Sphinx - page 31

D. 1. false
   2. true
   3. false
   4. false
   5. false
   6. false
   7. false

F. 1. has
   2. has
   3. has
   4. have
   5. have
   6. has
   7. have
   8. have

G. 1. lion
   2. pyramids
   3. ancient
   4. huge
   5. king
   6. long
   7. workers
   8. behind

7. Ngorongoro Game Preserve - page 37

D. 1. No way!
   2. No way!
   3. You bet!
   4. No way!
   5. You bet!
   6. No way!
   7. You bet!
   8. You bet! (No way?)

Answers

F. 1. We are going to go on a safari.
   2. I am going to see many animals.
   3. My friend is going to take many pictures.
   4. Are you going to come with us?
   5. Where are we going to stay?
   6. What are we going to do?
   7. When are we going to go?
   8. Who is going to pay for the safari?

G. 1. safari
   2. crater
   3. volcano
   4. anthropologist
   5. Early man
   6. bones
   7. found
   8. wildlife

8. Petra - page 43

D. 1. I don't think so.
   2. I don't think so.
   3. I don't think so.
   4. I think so, too.
   5. I think so, too.
   6. I don't thnk so.
   7. I think so, too.

F. 1. what
   2. where
   3. who, where
   4. when
   5. when
   6. what
   7. why
   8. who, where

G. 1. traders
   2. tribes
   3. busy
   4. buy, sell
   5. side, mountain
   6. unusual
   7. center, goods
   8. tombs

9. St. Basil's Cathedral - page 49

D. 1. Yes, that's true.
   2. No, that isn't true.
   3. No, that isn't true.
   4. No, that isn't true.
   5. Yes, that's true.
   6. No, that isn't true.
   7. Yes, that's true.
   8. No, that isn't true.

F. 1. my
   2. your
   3. her
   4. his
   5. our
   6. their
   7. your

G. 1. historical, including
   2. celebrated
   3. insane
   4. Terrible
   5. killed
   6. czar
   7. victory

10. The Taj Mahal - page 55

D. 1. Yes, you're right about that.
   2. No, you're wrong about that.
   3. No, you're wrong about that.
   4. No, you're wrong abut that.
   5. No, you're wrong about that.
   6. Yes, you're right about that.
   7. Yes, you're right about that.
   8. Yes, you're right about that.

F. 1. Yes, I went by plane.
   2. Yes, I saw the Taj Mahal.
   3. Yes, I had a guide.
   4. Yes, I took pictures.
   5. Yes, I visited friends.
   6. Yes, I looked at the gardens.
   7. Yes, I ate Indian food.
   8. Yes, I slept in a hotel.

Where in the World...

G. 1. gardens
   2. emperor
   3. remember
   4. died
   5. forever
   6. memorial, River
   7. incredible
   8. marble

11. Mount Everest - page 61

D. 1. That's wrong.
   2. That's right.
   3. That's wrong.
   4. That's wrong.
   5. That's wrong.
   6. That's right
   7. That's wrong.

F. 1. Do
   2. Does
   3. Do
   4. Do
   5. Do
   6. Does
   7. Does

G. 1. dangerous
   2. weather, try
   3. air, thin
   4. snowstorm
   5. guide
   6. border

12. The Potala Palace - page 67

D. 1. Tibet
   2. a museum
   3. over 1,000
   4. 7th century
   5. the leader of Tibetan Buddhists
   6. in exile in India
   7. The Dalai Lama

F. 1. was
   2. wasn't
   3. Was
   4. were
   5. Weren't
   6. were
   7. was
   8. was

G. 1. religion
   2. culture
   3. leader
   4. exile
   5. political
   6. palace
   7. jewels
   8. economic

13. The Terra Cotta Warriors - page 73

D. 1. No, that's false.
   2. Yes, that's true.
   3. No, that's false.
   4. No, that's false.
   5. No, that's false
   6. Yes, that's true.
   7. Yes, that's true.
   8. No, that's false.

F.   warriors, soldiers, armies
     emperors, cities, countries
     horses, places, sizes
     people, women, men

G. 1. Warriors
   2. horses, soldiers
   3. army
   4. fight
   5. life-size
   6. baked
   7. underground
   8. buried

14. The Great Wall - page 79

D. 1. Yes, exactly!
2. Sorry, you're wrong.
3. Sorry, you're wrong.
4. Sorry, you're wrong.
5. Yes, exactly!
6. Yes, exactly!
7. Yes, exactly!
8. Sorry, you're wrong.

F. 1. Are you going to visit China?
2. Is he going to like China?
3. Are you going to see the Great Wall?
4. Are they going to go with friends?
5. Is she going to travel by train?
6. Are they going to walk along the Wall?

G. 1. Wall
2. winds
3. Sea, Province
4. space
5. finish
6. workers, worked
7. way
8. west

15. Mount Fuji - page 85

D. 1. I don't think that's right.
2. I don't think that's right.
3. I think that's right.
4. I don't think that's right.
5. I think that's right.
6. I don't think that's right.
7. I think that's right.
8. I don't think that's right.

F. 1. This
2. These
3. This
4. These
5. These
6. This
7. These
8. This

G. 1. stay
2. trip
3. breathe
4. watch
5. sacred
6. overnight, come up
7. fresh
8. cone

16. Angkor Wat - page 91

D. 1. Yes, in fact, it is.
2. Actually, it isn't.
3. Actually, it isn't.
4. Yes, in fact, it is.
5. Yes, in fact, it is.
6. Actually, it isn't.
7. Actually, it isn't.

F. 1. Angkor Wat is large, isn't it?
2. It is a temple, isn't it?
3. It was a capital city, wasn't it?
4. It's on the flag, isn't it?
5. It was built in the 1100s, wasn't it?
6. It's unusual, isn't it?
7. It was in the Khmer Kingdom, wasn't it?

G. 1. capital
2. flag
3. Kingdom
4. proud
5. stone
6. capital
7. carvngs
8. stories, history

17. The Great Barrier Reef - page 97

D. 1. D, Australia
   2. F, coral (or barrier)
   3. G, millions
   4. H, 1,250 miles
   5. C, millions of years
   6. B, colorful
   7. A. biggest in the world
   8. E, Australians, tourists

F. 1. doesn't
   2. don't
   3. doesn't
   4. don't
   5. don't
   6. doesn't
   7. doesn't

G. 1. islands
   2. shell, coral
   3. reef, barrier
   4. formed
   5. surface
   6. Divers
   7. coast
   8. remains
   9. colorful, fantastic

18. Hawaii Volcanoes National Park - page 103

D. 1. Yes, I agree.
   2. No, I disagree.
   3. No, I disagee.
   4. Yes, I agree.
   5. Yes, I agree.
   6. No, I disagree,
   7. No, I disagree.
   8. No, I disagree.

F. 1. There are two active volcanoes.
   2. There is red, hot lava.
   3. Are there many campers?
   4. There are many visitors.
   5. Is there a public park on Hawaii?
   6. Are there many islands?
   7. There are many hikers in the park.

G. 1. lava
   2. active
   3. bubbles, flows
   4. hike, camp
   5. gifts, pray
   6. public
   7. volcanoes

19. Easter Island - page 109

D. 1. Yes, of course!
   2. Yes, of course!
   3. No, not really!
   4. No, not really!
   5. No, not really!
   6. Yes, of course!
   7. No, not really!
   8. Yes, of course!

F. 1. any
   2. any
   3. Some
   4. Some
   5. Some
   6. any
   7. some
   8. any

G. 1. strange
   2. mystery
   3. Others
   4. The rest
   5. isolated, about
   6. Approximately
   7. belongs to
   8. depends on

20. Antarctica - page 115

D. 1. No, that's not right at all!
2. No, that's not right at all!
3. Yes, that's right!
4. No, that's not right at all!
5. Yes, that's right!
6. Yes, that's right!
7. No, that's not right at all!
8. No, that's not right at all!

F. 1. In fact, it's the driest place.
2. In fact, it's the windiest place.
3. If fact it's the coldest place.
4. In fact, it's the darkest place.
5. In fact it's the highest place.
6. In fact, it's the loneliest place.
7. In fact, it's the iciest place.

G. 1. explorer
2. continent
3. froze
4. penguin
5. covered, sheet
6. surrounds
7. lonely
8. Seals

21. The Amazon Rainforest - page 121

D. 1. Yes, that's certainly true.
2. Yes, that's certainly true.
3. No, that's definitely wrong.
4. No, that's definitely wrong
5. No, that's definitely wrong
6. No, that's definitely wrong
7. Yes, that's certainly true.

F. 1. Is she taking photos?
2. Are they cutting trees now?
3. Is the forest getting smaller?
4. Are people clearing the land?
5. Are we looking at animals?
6. Am I leaving with you?
7. Is the forest growing fast?

G. 1. dense
2. clearing, cattle
3. Earth, planets
4. shrinking
5. fast
6. breathe, lungs
7. grow
8. healthy
9. Loggers, wood

22. Machu Picchu - page 127

D. 1. This sentence is not OK.
2. This sentence is OK.
3. This sentence is not OK.
4. This sentence is not OK.
5. This sentence is not OK.
6. This sentence is not OK.
7. This sentence is OK.

F. 1. The Inca weren't Spanish.
2. Machu Picchu wasn't a country.
3. Machu Picchu wasn't a Spanish city.
4. The Inca weren't Brazilians.
5. Machu Picchu wasn't a park
6. The builders weren't the Maya.

G. 1. place
2. lost
3. culture
4. Perhaps, ceremonies
5. sky, close
6. popular
7. attracts

23. The Galapagos Islands -
page 133
D. 1. H, are in the Pacific.
   2. D, from the coast.
   3. G, by a volcano.
   4. A, cannot fly.
   5. F, for fish.
   6. E, are huge.
   7. B, visit the islands.
   8. C, is a threat.

F. 1. There are 13 main islands.
   2. They are 600 miles from the coast.
   3. There are many strange animals there.
   4. There are hundreds of tortoises on the islands.
   5. They are huge.
   6. There are thousands of lizards.
   7. They are called iguanas.

G. 1. fly
   2. weigh
   3. lizard, powerful
   4. bother
   5. threatens
   6. developed
   7. evolution
   8. unique

24. The Panama Canal - page 139
D. 1. E, two oceans
   2. F, about 50 miles
   3. G, France
   4. B, 1880
   5. H, 1914
   6. A, thousands
   7. C, from malaria and accidents
   8. D, Panama

F. 1. Yes, it did.
   2. No, it didn't.
   3. Yes, they did.
   4. Yes, they did.
   5. Yes, they did.
   6. No, it didn't.
   7. No, it didn't.

G. 1. connects
   2. expensive, construction
   3. accidents
   4. use
   5. dream
   6. failed, complete
   7. save
   8. Malaria

25. Chichen Itza - page 145
D. 1. No, that's incorrect.
   2. Yes, that's correct.
   3. Yes, that's correct.
   4. No, that's incorrect.
   5. Yes, that's correct.
   6. Yes, that's correct.

F. 1. Were the Maya good architects?
   2. Was it built a long time ago?
   3. Was El Castillo a Spanish church?
   4. Were the Maya Native Americans?
   5. Was the writing system complex?
   6. Was Chichen Itza a city?
   7. Were the Maya also in Central America?
   8. Was Chichen Itza established in 1500 C.E.?

G. 1. complex, sysem
   2. peninsula
   3. established
   4. skillful
   5. Descendants
   6. ceremonies
   7. calendar, accurate

26. The Grand Canyon - page 151

D. 1. I don't agree with that.
   2. I agree with that.
   3. I don't agree with that.
   4. I don't agree with that.
   5. I don't agree with that.
   6. I agree with that.
   7. I don't agree with that.

F. 1. The river is <u>at</u> the bottom.
   2. I want to go <u>in</u> the afternoon.
   3. Let's go <u>at</u> three o'clock.
   4. Let's go <u>on</u> Monday.
   5. I want to go <u>in</u> the evening.
   6. I want to go <u>at</u> night.
   7. I want to go <u>in</u> the summer.
   8. You can ride <u>on</u> a mule.
   9. You can raft <u>on</u> the river.

G. 1. majestic
   2. long, deep, wide
   3. side
   4. ride, mule
   5. raft
   6. expedition
   7. bottom

27. Golden Gate National Recreation Area - page 157

D. 1. That's true.
   2. That's false.
   3. That's ttrue.
   4. That's false.
   5. That's true.
   6. That's false.
   7. That's true.
   8. That's false.

F. 1. She is going to San Francisco.
   2. He is going with her.
   3. They are going.
   4. We are tourists.
   5. It is beautiful.
   6. Are you on the bridge?
   7. Yes, I am.

G. 1. prison
   2. narrow, between
   3. bay
   4. bridge
   5. park
   6. gate
   7. urban
   8. infamous

28. Yellowstone National Park - page 163

D. 1. That isn't true.
   2. That isn't true.
   3. That isn't true.
   4. That isn't true.
   5. That's true.
   6. That isn't true.
   7. That's true.

F. 1. that
   2. that, those
   3. those
   4. That
   5. Those
   6. those
   7. those
   8. that

G. 1. overcrowded
   2. acres
   3. manages, sites
   4. enjoy, outdoors
   5. fish, lake
   6. snowmobiles
   7. seashore
   8. forest

29. Niagara Falls - page 169

D. 1. Yes, that's quite true.
2. That's not true at all.
3. Yes, that's quite true.
4. That's not true at all.
5. Yes, that's quite true.
6. Yes, that's quite true.
7. That's not true at all.
8. Yes, that's quite true.

F. 1. I'm a student
2. He's a teacher.
3. We're tourists.
4. They're on their honeymoon.
5. You're from China.
6. She's at Niagara Falls.
7. Mary's in New York.

G. 1. inland waterway, share
2. honeymooners
3. survived
4. Daredevils, barrel
5. electricity
6. loud
7. lights
8. halfway

30. Washington, D.C. - page 175

D. 1. Yes, it is.
2. No, there aren't.
3. Yes, it does.
4. No, it isn't.
5. No, it isn't.
6. No, it doesn't.

F. 1. From one end to anoter there are many museums.
2. The Capitol is at one end of the Mall.
3. The Washington Monument is partway down the mall.
4. Congress makes laws for the people.
5. Along the sides are three war memorials.
6. Not far from the capitol is the Supreme Court.
7. On top of the building is statue.
8. You can walk inside the capitol and look around.

G. 1. laws
2. Congress
3. Monument, landmark
4. Along
5. meets
6. end
7. Mall
8. look around, speeches

Answers   **199**

Other Pro Lingua Books of Interest for Beginning-Level Learners

ENGLISH INTERPLAY: SURVIVING. An integrated skills text for absolute beginners. Lots of pair and small group work. A variety of activities: exchanges, rituals, operations, games, rhymes. Includes grammar notes, pronunciation practice. Features ten units focused on survival language. Separate TEACHER'S BOOK is available. Includes all the student material plus suggestions and instructions for the teacher and additional resource material.

FROM SOUND TO SENTENCE. A basic and fun literacy and spelling workbook based on a phonics approach supplemented by sight words. From *Pat's pet bat* to *the lazy zebra and the crazy ox.* Supplemented with three CDs.

SUPERPHONIC BINGO. 15 photocopyable games following the presentation of sound-letter combinations in *From Sound to Sentence.* Each game has eight different cards and two incomplete cards.

THE READ AND LEARN SERIES: READ 50, READ 75, READ 100, READ 125.
(In *Read 50* the readings average 50 words in length, etc.) Each book has 40 readings with short exercises. The readings are in a variety of formats: descriptive paragraphs, emails, blogs, graphs, maps, posters, comic strips, etc. The topics focus on "our global village." A CD is available for each book.

The Sanchez Family. A brief integrated-skills text that teaches the present progressive, the going-to future, and the simple past to real beginners. The students learn literacy skills, 70 high-frequency verbs, and survival vocabulary. Teacher's Guide has extra copyable activities.

INDEX CARD GAMES FOR ESL. A photocopyable teacher resource with dozens of games, from easy to difficult. Copy, cut, and paste on index cards.

PLAY 'N' TALK. A teacher resource collection of communicative games for young, beginning level learners. Photocopyable material is included.

THE INTERACTIVE TUTORIAL. 57 photocopyable activities for adult learners, beginning to low-intermediate level. Designed for one-on-one tutoring, but easily adaptable for use with small groups. Most activities can be used with younger learners.

Pro Lingua Associates
P.O. Box 1348
Brattleboro, VT 05302 U.S.A.

Orders: (800) 366-4775
Inquiries/Advice Hotline (802) 257-7779
FAX: (802) 257- 5117
Email: Info@ProLinguaAssociates.com
Webstore: www.ProLinguaAssociates.com